DATE DUE

DEC 0 4 2013			

Demco, Inc. 38-293

HANTAVIRUS PULMONARY SYNDROME

Anthrax

Avian Flu

Botulism

Campylobacteriosis

Cholera

Ebola

Encephalitis

Escherichia coli
Infections

Gonorrhea

Hantavirus
Pulmonary Syndrome

Hepatitis

Herpes

HIV/AIDS

Infectious Fungi

Influenza

Legionnaires' Disease

Leprosy

Lyme Disease

Mad Cow Disease
(Bovine Spongiform
Encephalopathy)

Malaria

Meningitis

Mononucleosis

Pelvic Inflammatory
Disease

Plague

Polio

Salmonella

SARS

Smallpox

Streptococcus
(Group A)

*Staphylococcus
aureus* Infections

Syphilis

Toxic Shock
Syndrome

Tuberculosis

Tularemia

Typhoid Fever

West Nile Virus

DEADLY DISEASES AND EPIDEMICS

HANTAVIRUS PULMONARY SYNDROME

Stephanie J. Leuenroth

FOUNDING EDITOR
The Late **I. Edward Alcamo**
Distinguished Teaching Professor of Microbiology,
SUNY Farmingdale

FOREWORD BY
David Heymann
World Health Organization

CHELSEA HOUSE
PUBLISHERS
An imprint of Infobase Publishing

Hantavirus Pulmonary Syndrome

Copyright © 2006 by Infobase Publishing

Chelsea House
An imprint of Infobase Publishing
132 West 31st Street
New York NY 10001

Library of Congress Cataloging-in-Publication Data

Leuenroth, Stephanie, 1972–
   Hantavirus pulmonary syndrome/Stephanie Leuenroth.
     p. cm.—(Deadly diseases and epidemics)
   Includes bibliographical references.
   ISBN 0-7910-8676-3
   1. Hantavirus pulmonary syndrome—Juvenile literature. 2. Hantaviruses—Juvenile literature. I. Title. II. Series.
   RC147.H36L48 2005
   616.9'18—dc22   2005026623

Series design by Terry Mallon
Cover design by Keith Trego

Printed in the United States of America

Bang 21C 10 9 8 7 6 5 4 3 2 1

Table of Contents

Foreword

In the 1960s, many of the infectious diseases that had terrorized generations were tamed. After a century of advances, the leading killers of Americans both young and old were being prevented with new vaccines or cured with new medicines. The risk of death from pneumonia, tuberculosis (TB), meningitis, influenza, whooping cough, and diphtheria declined dramatically. New vaccines lifted the fear that summer would bring polio, and a global campaign was on the verge of eradicating smallpox worldwide. New pesticides like DDT cleared mosquitoes from homes and fields, thus reducing the incidence of malaria, which was present in the southern United States and which remains a leading killer of children worldwide. New technologies produced safe drinking water and removed the risk of cholera and other water-borne diseases. Science seemed unstoppable. Disease seemed destined to all but disappear.

But the euphoria of the 1960s has evaporated.

The microbes fought back. Those causing diseases like TB and malaria evolved resistance to cheap and effective drugs. The mosquito developed the ability to defuse pesticides. New diseases emerged, including AIDS, Legionnaires, and Lyme disease. And diseases which had not been seen in decades re-emerged, as the hantavirus did in the Navajo Nation in 1993. Technology itself actually created new health risks. The global transportation network, for example, meant that diseases like West Nile virus could spread beyond isolated regions and quickly become global threats. Even modern public health protections sometimes failed, as they did in 1993 in Milwaukee, Wisconsin, resulting in 400,000 cases of the digestive system illness cryptosporidiosis. And, more recently, the threat from smallpox, a disease believed to be completely eradicated, has returned along with other potential bioterrorism weapons such as anthrax.

The lesson is that the fight against infectious diseases will never end.

In our constant struggle against disease, we as individuals have a weapon that does not require vaccines or drugs, and that is the warehouse of knowledge. We learn from the history of science that "modern" beliefs can be wrong. In this series of books, for example, you will learn that diseases like syphilis were once thought to be caused by eating potatoes. The invention of the microscope set science on the right path. There are more positive lessons from history. For example, smallpox was eliminated by vaccinating everyone who had come in contact with an infected person. This "ring" approach to smallpox control is still the preferred method for confronting an outbreak, should the disease be intentionally reintroduced.

At the same time, we are constantly adding new drugs, new vaccines, and new information to the warehouse. Recently, the entire human genome was decoded. So too was the genome of the parasite that causes malaria. Perhaps by looking at the microbe and the victim through the lens of genetics we will be able to discover new ways to fight malaria, which remains the leading killer of children in many countries.

Because of advances in our understanding of such diseases as AIDS, entire new classes of anti-retroviral drugs have been developed. But resistance to all these drugs has already been detected, so we know that AIDS drug development must continue.

Education, experimentation, and the discoveries that grow out of them are the best tools to protect health. Opening this book may put you on the path of discovery. I hope so, because new vaccines, new antibiotics, new technologies, and, most importantly, new scientists are needed now more than ever if we are to remain on the winning side of this struggle against microbes.

David Heymann
Executive Director
Communicable Diseases Section
World Health Organization
Geneva, Switzerland

1

The Discovery and History of Hantavirus

The raw beauty and vast expanse of the Four Corners region of the southwestern United States was the setting for a new epidemic in May of 1993. A young Navajo man was rushed to the emergency room after experiencing difficulty breathing; he ultimately died from **respiratory** distress. This mysterious illness would probably have been classified as another unexplained respiratory syndrome if it was not for the fact that his fiancée had died just days earlier of the same symptoms. This observation set into motion a series of inquiries, such as: Were there others who suffered the same fate? Could the cause be an agent that is **infectious**? It was quickly discovered that there were five additional cases, and that these, too, were young healthy individuals. In all five cases, as with the young man and his fiancée, death occurred following acute respiratory failure. Laboratory tests done on these patients ruled out infectious agents such as those that cause bubonic plague, influenza, pneumonia, as well as many other common bacterial or viral agents. With the sudden onset of unexplained deaths in this small region of the Southwest, local authorities decided it was time to contact specialized scientists trained in the study of infectious disease outbreaks at the Centers for Disease Control and Prevention (CDC).

IDENTIFYING THE SIN NOMBRE STRAIN

A team of medical doctors, **epidemiologists**, virologists, and molecular biologists was quickly mobilized to find the source of this mysterious disease. The clinical symptoms all started with fever, severe muscle aches, and possibly nausea and vomiting—all very typical of what might be expected from the flu. Within days, however, symptoms became worse, with fluid building in the lungs, making it increasingly difficult for the victims to breathe. The danger in this progression was that the symptoms went from bad to worse in a matter of hours, with acute **pulmonary** failure and death the frequent outcome. Having this information, the investigators decided that blood samples from patients would be tested for reactivity to known **viruses,** while at the same time other explanations such as poisoning would also be explored. Visits to the homes of the patients diagnosed with the mysterious illness revealed no common source of poison; however, results from patient samples led to a break in the case. When looking for specific **antibodies** present in blood, the researchers found one viral strain that showed a positive result. The virus identified was the Puumala hanta-virus, a strain **endemic** to Europe that produced mild effects on the kidney. Although this virus did not cause the symptoms that were observed in the Four Corners region (Figure 1.1), the

POLYMERASE CHAIN REACTION (PCR)

"PCR has transformed molecular biology through vastly extending the capacity to identify, manipulate and reproduce DNA. It makes abundant what was once scarce—the genetic material required for experimentations."

Paul Rabinow
Making PCR, A Story of Biotechnology,
University of Chicago Press, 1996

The Polymerase Chain Reaction (PCR) can best be described as a procedure in which to amplify specific stretches of

nucleic acid for the purposes of genetic identification. Kary B. Mullis is credited with the invention of PCR in 1985 and this technique hinges upon the use of a very specialized enzyme known as a **polymerase**. A polymerase by definition is a **protein** that can actively form and repair DNA or **RNA**. Due to the fact that PCR requires high temperatures to separate double stranded DNA, a highly specialized and heat stable polymerase was required for this process. Such a polymerase was found from a bacterial strain found in thermal springs called *Thermus aquaticus*, and its enzyme was hence called Taq polymerase. With this new reagent in hand, the process of rapidly amplifying small stretches of DNA in a tube could begin. To start with, a piece of template DNA is needed, such as that purified from a blood test. The next requirement is a set of DNA **primers** (or short stretches of complementary DNA) that will serve as a starting point to copy the region of DNA that is of interest. If the target sequence contains a region that the primer can bind to, then that specific piece of DNA will be copied. When PCR begins, the temperature is raised and the double stranded DNA template separates. This is followed by lowering the temperature so the primers can bind, followed by copying the remainder of the DNA fragment. This process is repeated many times in cycles, where each cycle produces an **exponential** growth of copies of the DNA. Upon completion of this 'chain reaction' (usually a few hours), the DNA sequence originally targeted will be amplified more than 1,000,000 times. This process allows for the identification of any piece of DNA from any organism and is routinely used in research laboratories, infectious and genetic disease research, as well as in forensics.

Figure 1.1 The Four Corners region of the southwestern United States, named so because Utah, Colorado, Arizona, and New Mexico all converge at one point. This was the region of the U.S. that the first HPS outbreak occurred in 1993.

scientists decided to pursue the investigation by using a new technique called the **polymerase chain reaction**, or PCR.

Stuart Nicol, a virologist at the CDC, began by making small **DNA** fragments called primers that were found within at least two of the already known strains of hantavirus. The hope was that this new **pathogen** was another member of the already identified hantavirus family and that these DNA primers would produce a positive test result. As new cases of this deadly disease were being reported, the results from the tests became clear: The researchers were indeed dealing with a new, yet unknown, form of hantavirus. Within weeks of this discovery, antibodies were produced to identify and screen patient samples for the presence of this new Sin Nombre (which means "no name" in Spanish) strain of hantavirus. **Pathologists** examining tissues from patients afflicted with this new disease found that the virus was accumulating in the **capillaries** of the lung. When this happened, the capillaries were damaged. This caused fluid to leak into the lung and resulted in respiratory distress. It was known that other hanta-viruses existed around the world, but they produced different symptoms and had a lower **mortality** rate. The Sin Nombre strain was different in that its effects were seen much faster after infection, it was more lethal, and its primary targets were the lungs and not the kidneys. The mystery of the cause of this new illness was now solved. The next question was: Where did it come from?

CLUES FROM THE NAVAJO

When epidemiologists began talking to Navajo elders, it became evident that this disease progression had been seen in years past. Every spring, when cases of pulmonary distress were seen, they were always preceded by several factors: a period of heavy precipitation; an abundance of grain, berries, and piñon nuts; and an explosion in the rodent population. This information made sense, as mice and rats were known to spread the other hantaviruses to humans. In order to prove this theory, a variety of rodents were trapped around the homes of people who contracted the Sin Nombre strain and tested for the presence of the virus. More than 1,000 rodents were trapped, the most common was the deer mouse (*Peromyscus maniculatus*) that often resides in woodpiles, barns, and homes (Figure 1.2). Tests showed that 30% of these deer mice were carriers of the new

Figure 1.2 The deer mouse (*Peromyscus maniculatus*) is the predominant carrier of the Sin Nombre strain of hantavirus.

strain of hantavirus. The pieces of this puzzle began falling into place: The deer mouse population had increased over 10 times its normal size due to an abundance of food, which led to increased contact between rodents and people, which further resulted in the increased number of pulmonary distress cases.

NEW WORLD STRAINS OF HANTAVIRUS

The new strain of hantavirus discovered in the Four Corners region of the United States was called Sin Nombre and the illness it caused became known as hantavirus pulmonary syndrome (HPS). What became clear after this outbreak was that there were many other New World hantaviruses present in both North and South America that were also causing HPS (Figure 1.3). Years before the 1993 outbreak, scientists were already trapping and testing rodents in the United States as possible carriers for hantavirus. As early as 1982, two hantavirus virologists, Richard Yanagihara and D. Carleton Gajdusek, announced the discovery of the first known North American hantavirus, the Prospect Hill strain. Although there was no **correlation** between this strain and any known diseases, there was concern that this **hemorrhagic** virus may infect individuals who routinely have contact with rodents. Additional studies funded by the U.S. Army Medical Research Institute of Infectious Diseases (USAMRIID) found that rats in Baltimore, Maryland and other cities tested positive for yet another known strain of hantavirus, this time the Seoul strain. It was becoming increasingly evident that hantavirus was present in the United States, that the strains and symptoms of infection were different from viruses of the same family found in Europe and Asia, and that rodents harboring these New World viruses were probably present throughout the Americas.

The Sin Nombre virus was the cause of first known outbreak, but it was certainly not the first time HPS was seen. Lung tissue samples from patients who had died from unexplained lung disease or acute respiratory distress were examined for signs of hantavirus infection. Results showed that many of these unexplained cases could now in fact be ruled as HPS. Additionally, a specialized method of examining frozen tissue samples—called **immunohistochemistry**—revealed that the earliest known HPS case was a Utah man in 1959. Since the 1993 Four Corners outbreak, HPS has been reported in other areas of the United States, and other Sin Nombre-like strains have been identified with different rodent hosts. Louisiana was home to the Bayou strain carried by the rice rat; the Black

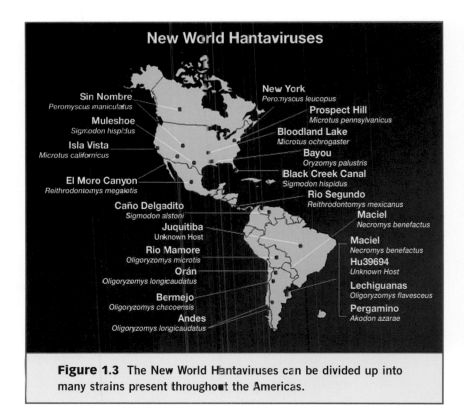

Figure 1.3 The New World Hantaviruses can be divided up into many strains present throughout the Americas.

Creek Canal strain was linked to a man in Florida and was carried by the cotton rat; and a case in New York was tied to the white-footed mouse and named the New York-1 virus. South America and Canada have also had cases of HPS reported from a variety of New World hantaviruses. Although these New World strains differ from the Old World strain in that they are relatively rare, they may ultimately be more devastating.

OLD WORLD HAANTAN VIRUSES

There are many Old World hantavirus strains, not all of which directly cause a disease. The earliest records describing the classic symptoms of a hantavirus infection were first written down in Chinese medical texts over 1,000 years ago, thereby establishing the existence of hantavirus over many centuries.

IMMUNOHISTOCHEMISTRY (IHC)

Immunohistochemistry is a technique that is used to detect specific antigens from a patient tissue sample, such as in the identification of hantavirus in the lung. These tissue samples must be specially prepared such as having to be frozen or embedded into a block of wax before they can be cut into fractions of a millimeter. Antibodies, which are specialized proteins made by the immune system to recognize a wide variety of **antigens** (anything that can invoke an immune response), are then added onto the tissue sample. If the antigen of interest is present, such as a viral protein, the antibody will find it and form a stable interaction. By analogy, this interaction can be thought of two pieces of a puzzle that are stuck together. Once this antibody-antigen complex has formed, an additional reagent that results in a color change (seen as a brown colored stain) can detect this binding. If the antigen of interest is not present, the antibody will not bind and will simply be washed away. In this way, patient samples can be screened in large numbers and positive or negative results are easily identified. In the example shown in the figure, a lung tissue sample was taken from a patient who later died of hantavirus pulmonary syndrome. The tissue was stained for a specific viral antigen and brown colored spots are observed in vascular **endothelial** cells lining the alveoli of the lung. This indicated that the patient was indeed positive for hantavirus infection. The blue color simply stains all cells and represents normal lung tissue. IHC is a useful procedure used by research laboratories as well as by pathologists in order to identify targets of medical relevance.

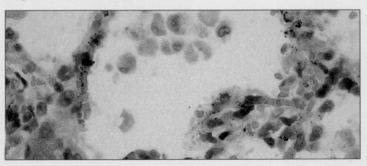

The classification of each virus is dependent upon its geographical location, its native rodent host, and its ability to bring about clinical symptoms. Many of the Old World viruses cause hemorrhagic fever with **renal** syndrome (HFRS); these include the Hantaan, Dobrava, and Seoul strains. Typically, these are the most severe strains, having a mortality rate of up to 15%. These strains can be found throughout Asia, the Balkans, and Europe. Additionally, a milder **nephric** epidemic, with a mortality rate usually under 1%, was first reported in Sweden. The cause of this outbreak was not discovered until 1980, when the virus (later named Puumala after a lake in Finland) was isolated from a vole. As trading routes were established from the Old World to the New World, rats and mice are believed to have stowed away on these ships and thus given the opportunity to spread hantavirus worldwide. Over time, through genetic **mutation** of these hantaviruses, the strains that cause HPS evolved. Of the cases of hantavirus infection that occurred around the globe between 1993 and 2000, there have been 550 cases of HPS in the Americas versus approximately 150,000 cases of other hantaviral infection. While, HPS continues to have the highest mortality rate (near 40%), it is fortunate that the number of cases is relatively small.

A MILITARY DISEASE

Historically, hantavirus infections have been reported within the realm of military maneuvers and battles within Europe and Asia. During both World War I (1914–1918) and World War II (1939–1945), there were reports of "trench nephritis" affecting French, British, and German troops, although no known infectious agent was identified. During the Korean War (1950–1953), over 300 United Nations troops developed Korean hemorrhagic fever (KHF), which was characterized by multi-organ dysfunction, hemorrhages, and shock. Although the mortality rate of KHF was 5 to 10%, it was one of the most severe forms of hantavirus infection. It was not until 23 years after the end of the Korean War that the cause of KHF was identified and isolated from the Korean striped field mouse. The virus was named "hantavirus" after the location of the battlefront and the cases of reported KHF: the Hantaan River, which runs near the border of North and South Korea. Since the time of the Korean War, other outbreaks of Haantan-like virus epidemics were reported in military personnel from Yugoslavia and Greece. In 1990, several years before the Four Corners outbreak, U.S. troops doing maneuvers in Germany came down with HFRS. This was attributed to rodent infestation of the area where the troops were stationed. Hantavirus is transmitted by aerosolized excretions from rodents; any time their natural habitat is disturbed, there is a danger that the virus may become airborne. Military personnel have therefore been at increased risk for contracting this class of virus, since battles and training exercises are carried out in the field where wild rodents make their home.

CASES REPORTED SINCE 1993

Hantavirus pulmonary syndrome (HPS) became recognizable after the 1993 outbreak in the U.S. Southwest. Since that time, other strains and cases of the illness have been identified. As of July 2005, there have been 396 reported cases of HPS with an overall mortality rate of 36% within the United States alone. As reported by the CDC, 62% of the cases have been in males, with an age range spanning 10 to 75 years (average of 38). Rodents screened all across the country, even within cities, have turned up positive as hantavirus carriers. HPS cases have been reported in 31 states, with the fewest cases in the Northeast (New York, Rhode Island, Vermont, Connecticut, New Hampshire) and the highest incidence reported in the western United States (Figure 1.4). Of the 396 confirmed HPS illnesses, only 7 were a direct result of the New York, Bayou, or Black Creek strains, with the remainder being due to Sin Nombre infection. Hundreds of additional cases of HPS have also been reported

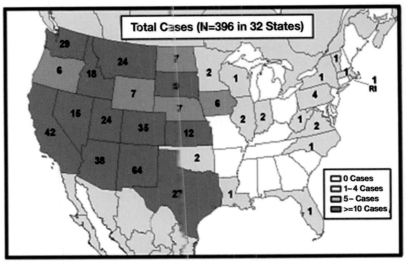

Hantavirus Pulmonary Syndrome Cases
By State of Residence, United States – July 6, 2005

Total Cases (N=396 in 32 States)

0 Cases
1–4 Cases
5– Cases
>=10 Cases

Three cases were reported with unknown state of residence.

Figure 1.4 The number of HPS cases reported by state of residence (does not reflect the state in which viral infection occurred) as of July 2005. The majority of cases are localized to the southwestern United States.

in Canada, Brazil, Chile, Argentina, and Panama. Although HPS is relatively rare, new infections will continue to develop as people encounter rodents in their native habitats. Since the identification of HPS, however, medical professionals are now aware of the symptoms and have developed specialized tests for accurate identification of hantavirus. Encouragingly, early diagnosis and treatment have helped decrease the overall mortality rate from 50% in 1993 to 36% by 2005.

2

Hantavirus:
The Anatomy of a Pathogen

WHAT IS A VIRUS?

The word "virus," taken from the Latin word for "poison," was adopted in the late 1800s to describe a submicroscopic infectious particle. Viruses are intracellular parasites that are considered to be nonliving, as they rely on a host for all replicative functions. There are countless viruses that can infect anything from bacteria to plants and animals, and they all share two common characteristics: the presence of **nucleic acid** and a protein coat or **capsid** to protect it. One very important distinction between a virus and a cellular organism is that viruses are inert when outside of a host. Viruses do not grow, but are in fact assembled within the living host cell. Since viruses are parasites, they cause damage to or kill the cells they infect. This process induces cellular **pathology** that is ultimately responsible for disease. In plants, viral infections bring about low crop yields, stunted growth, or destruction of leaves or the root system. In animals and humans, viruses can cause a multitude of diseases ranging from the "common cold" and influenza, to smallpox, rabies, and even cancer.

Viruses can be classified based on the following characteristics: **morphology** (size and shape), chemical properties, **genome** structure and nucleic acid composition, protein expression, and biological properties (host preference and mode of transmission). Although viruses vary greatly in these characteristics, they all have a similar life cycle. The life cycle begins with the initiation stage, in which the virus must attach to and enter its host cell. The next stage is the replication phase, which involves the synthesis of DNA, RNA, and proteins. Next, the viruses are assembled and exit the cell during the release phase. This cycle repeats for as long as the virus has new target cells to infect or until the host organism can eliminate the virus.

BUNYAVIRIDAE FAMILY

Viral **taxonomy** is divided up into the categories of order, family, subfamily, genus, species, and strain. The Bunyaviridae family is the largest of all viruses, comprising five genera and over 300 species. The genera include Bunyavirus, Phlebovirus, Nairovirus, Tospovirus, and Hantavirus (Figure 2.1). In the example of HPS, the taxonomic classification for the virus responsible for the Four Corners outbreak would be a part of the Bunyaviridae family (the order for this family has not yet been designated), the hantavirus genus, and the Sin Nombre species. All members of the Bunyaviridae family are spherical (80 to 120 nm in size), contain single-stranded RNA, and have two **glycoproteins** (proteins that have sugar units attached to them) embedded in a lipid bilayer envelope (Figure 2.2). The envelope surrounds the protein coat and is derived from the host cell upon viral release. Additionally, Bunyaviruses can also assemble an elongated particle (110 to 120 nm in length) known as a spike that facilitates cellular entry.

The Bunyavirus genome is composed of three regions of circular RNA that are referred to as the L, M, and S segments. Each of these segments is responsible for encoding different

A PARTIAL HISTORY OF VIROLOGY

It was not until the 1800s that a virus was discovered as a separate infectious agent different from that of bacteria or other organisms. As viruses are much smaller than bacteria, it was difficult at the time to test for their presence or even know that they existed. All that was clear was that something that you could not see or touch or even grow by conventional means was making people, animals, and plants sick. Two respected scientists in the 1880s, Louis Pasteur and Robert Koch, devised the same principal idea of the "germ theory" of disease. Louis Pasteur, also made famous by introducing the process of pasteurization, did extensive work on rabies and called the infectious agent responsible for the disease a virus. Robert Koch went on to further describe the criteria needed for proof that a disease is caused by an infectious agent. These are known today as **Koch's Postulates** and are listed as follows:

1. The agent must be present in all cases of the disease.

2. The agent must be isolated from the host and grown in culture.

3. The disease must be reproduced when introduced into a susceptible healthy host.

4. The same agent must be found in the experimentally infected host.

In the 1890s, Russian botanist Dmitri Iwanowski was working on a project with diseased tobacco plants. He was able to show that extracts from a diseased plant when applied to a healthy plant could make it sick. What was striking is that he first passed the diseased plant extract through a filter that would prevent any bacteria from flowing through it. This showed that an agent smaller than a bacterial cell was able to transmit disease. This finding is considered to be the beginning of virology. In 1898, Iwanowski's work on the tobacco plant was repeated and confirmed by Martinus Beijerinick and the infectious agent was called the tobacco mosaic virus. Beijerinick also referred to the virus as *contagium vivum fluidum* or "soluble living germ," and helped to establish the current concept of the virus.

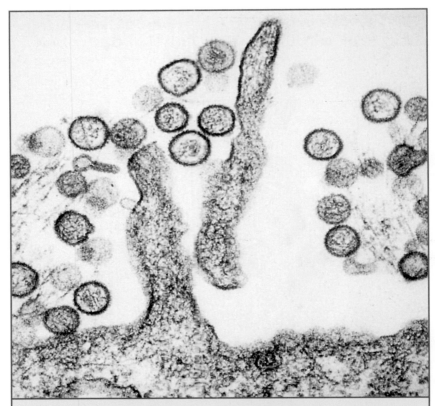

Figure 2.1 A transmission electron microscope (TEM) image of hantavirus (circular structures) budding from an infected cell.

proteins that are required for the assembly of new viruses. The majority of the viruses in this family can infect mammals; only the Tospovirus genus can infect plants. With the exception of hantaviruses—which require a rodent reservoir— Bunyaviridae viruses are transmitted by **arthropods** (a group of animals that includes mosquitoes, ticks, and fleas). Interestingly, the rodent or arthropod carriers of the viruses are not adversely affected and do not become ill. Some Bunyaviridae viruses are not known to infect humans, whereas others are the cause of such severe infections as Rift Valley fever, hemorrahagic fever, and HPS.

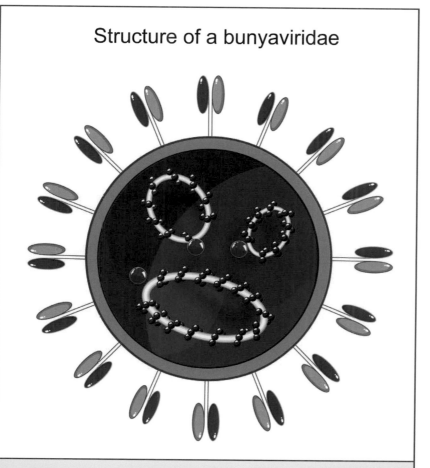

Figure 2.2 The hantavirus genome is comprised of single stranded RNA divided into the L, M, and S segments. Surrounding this genetic material is a protein coat, a lipid envelope, and protruding glycoproteins required for cellular entry.

THE HANTAVIRUS GENOME

In the Baltimore Classification of viral genomes, there are seven different groups broken down by how the virus replicates. The central premise is that all viruses must first generate a (+) strand mRNA to generate protein and then begin the process of genomic replication (Figure 2.3). As a result, the

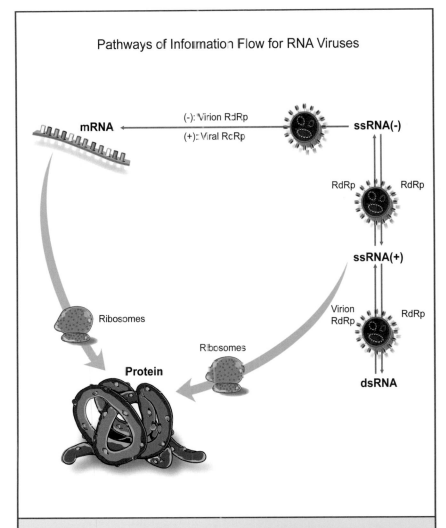

Figure 2.3 In order for protein to be produced, mRNA ((+) sense) must be used as a template. For hantaviral protein production, this process must first begin with the conversion of single stranded (-) sense RNA into mRNA and then on to protein.

classification system is based on the type of nucleic acid, if there are one or two strands of the genome, and if the strand (single-stranded) is in the 5' → 3' direction (known as (+)

sense), or in the 3' → 5' direction (known as (-) sense). The classification system is as follows:

I. Double-stranded DNA

II. Single-stranded (+) sense DNA

III. Double-stranded RNA

IV. Single-stranded (+) sense RNA

V. Single-stranded (-) sense RNA

VI. Single-stranded (+) sense RNA with a DNA intermediate

VII. Double-stranded DNA with an RNA intermediate

The hantavirus genome comprises single-stranded (-) sense RNA (category V.) and is divided into three segments known as L, M, and S for large, medium, and small. Each of these segments is covered by the protein known as the N protein and forms a helical nucleocapsid. The L segment is the largest at 6.5 kb (**kilobases**) and encodes a viral **transcriptase** or **polymerase** that converts the (-) sense genomic RNA into messenger RNA (mRNA), which can then be translated into protein. The transcriptase protein is also found associated with each segment of the genome in order to quickly initiate this process upon cellular entry. The M segment is approximately 3.6 kb and codes for a glycoprotein precursor that is cleaved into the G1 and G2 proteins that regulate viral entry into the cell. This region of the genome has the most variability between hantavirus species, as a change of even a single amino acid can result in differences in host specificity and pathogenicity. **Mutations** in this segment are most frequently due to copying errors by the viral RNA polymerase. The S segment is 1.7 kb and codes for the N protein that makes up the nucleocapsid. It is hypothesized that sufficient N protein must be present before viral RNA can be replicated and subsequently packaged into a new virus or **encapsidated.**

MECHANISMS OF CELLULAR ENTRY, REPLICATION, AND RELEASE

Every virus is specific in that it may only infect a certain species or even a certain cell type within an organism. This is referred

---

HERSHEY–CHASE BACTERIOPHAGE STUDIES

Until the experiments performed by Alfred D. Hershey and Martha Chase in 1952, the answer to the question of whether nucleic acid or protein was the genetic component of the cell was unknown. The design for their experiment was very elegant in that they used a simple system employing the bacteria *Escherichia coli* (*E. coli*) and a virus that infects this bacteria known as a bacteriophage (literally meaning "bacteria eater"). In this system, it was known that one part of the virus remained outside of the cell while the genetic component was injected inside the bacterium. To begin, two separate samples of bacteriophage were prepared: one sample had DNA labeled with radioactive phosphorus (^{32}P) and the second sample had protein labeled with radioactive sulfur (^{35}S). The purpose of the radioactivity was simply to use it as a tag to identify where the DNA or the protein would go upon infection into the host bacteria. Once the two samples of bacteriophage were prepared, they were allowed to separately infect bacteria and then the bacterial cells were spun in a blender to separate any virus material that remained outside of the cell. Next, the cells were spun down in a centrifuge and then both the bacterial mass and the extracellular solution were assayed for the presence of a radioactive signal. What they found was that the ^{35}S labeled protein remained outside of the cell and the ^{32}P labeled DNA was inside of the cell. This classic experiment concluded that DNA, and not protein, was the genetic material, and it paved the way for other scientists to solve the structure of DNA.

to as **viral tropism**. Some viruses can preferentially target humans while having no effect on other mammals, and vice versa. The question has been raised as to why there is such a degree of specificity for viral infection of a host. The answer lies with the proteins expressed by the virus, as well as the cellular receptors they recognize. The first step in cellular attachment or entry is accomplished when the virus successfully binds to its specific receptor (there may be one or more cellular targets). In the case of hantavirus, the known receptor for viral entry is a family of proteins known as the beta (β) integrins. These are large proteins present at the cell membrane that are involved in attachment to extracellular matrix proteins or to other cells. There may be multiple β-integrin isoforms expressed on a cell and some integrins that are only present on certain types of cells. Interestingly, all hantaviruses do not recognize the same β-integrin isoform. The pathogenic hantavirus strains (Hantaan, Seoul, Puumala, Sin Nombre, New York) use the β_3-integrin as a receptor while the nonpathogenic strains (Prospect Hill, Tula) recognize the β_1-integrin.

Once the virus has successfully attached to its cellular receptor, the penetration phase begins and is carried out by the cell. Upon viral binding, the cell internalizes the integrin receptor and viral complex in a process known as **endocytosis**. The virus and receptor are both present in a small vesicle (known as an **endosome)** inside the cell. This endosome will then fuse with a small, highly acidic sac called a **lysosome.** Normally, proteins are degraded by an acidic environment (low pH); however, the virus uses the low pH in the lysosome to its advantage by fusing with the lysosomal membrane. When this occurs, the virus (now without an envelope) is released into the cytoplasm and may begin production of viral mRNA.

Since the hantavirus genome is (-) sense stranded, the first step is transcription into the (+) sense mRNA that is then translated into viral protein. The proteins encoded by the hantavirus genome include the polymerase, the G1 and

G2 glycoproteins, and the N protein for the nucelocapsid. The Sin Nombre hantavirus has been shown to produce the highest mRNA copies of segment S (N protein), and the least amount of segment L (polymerase) within an infected cell. Production of a sufficient amount of N protein signals a switch from transcription of the viral genome to replication. The newly made (-) sense viral RNA is then bound by the L protein polymerase. This process is thought to occur in the

ELECTRON MICROSCOPY

In traditional light microscopy, viruses cannot be seen as they are too small. In 1931, Ernst Ruska and Max Knoll invented a powerful instrument called the electron microscope. With magnifications over 200,000x, we are now able to view incredible intricacies of cells, whole organisms such as fruit flies, and even viruses. Electron microscopy (EM) allows the virus to be viewed in terms of its outermost structure as well as determining the number of viral particles. Images of viruses budding from cells and even the surface structure of the capsid have been captured. There are two different types of EM known as transmission or TEM and scanning or SEM. Scanning EM allows one to see the surface features of an organism. To do this, the specimen must be coated in a metal such as gold. This technique has been used to view cells such as those of the immune system as well as to examine the structure of whole insects such as spiders, ticks, and fleas. Both SEM and TEM rely on a focused beam of electrons for imaging rather than visible light. While SEM can result in incredible detail and amazing imaging its degree of magnification is not as high as TEM. TEM is the primary EM used for viral imaging—the focused energy beam is able to penetrate the sample. In addition to viruses, bacteria, and fungi, cellular organelles can also be viewed with very fine resolution.

perinuclear region (around the nucleus) but the final assembly with G1 and G2 glycoproteins must occur at either the Golgi or plasma membrane. Preliminary research on the Sin Nombre hantavirus indicates that G1 and G2 assembly as well as viral budding occurs at the cell surface. The final viral envelope is derived from the cellular bilipid layer and simply buds off from the cell. All of the newly assembled progeny viruses are then free to target and infect other cells, and the process begins again.

3

Mechanisms of Cellular Destruction by Hantavirus

As intracellular parasites, viruses are not capable of replicating on their own and therefore always depend on a host for their survival. If viruses simply use cells for their intracellular machinery, why do they cause cellular destruction and disease? As it turns out, just as viruses differ in their nucleic acid genome, protein expression, and methods of cellular entry, they also differ in their ability to damage cells and induce pathogenesis. Some viruses can coexist with cells for a time without detection, whereas others cause cells to break open or induce overactivation of the immune response that in itself causes tissue damage.

HOW DOES A VIRUS KILL A CELL?

The viral life cycle begins with entry into the cell and ends with release of progeny virus. There are three different mechanisms for viral release into the intracellular environment. These are classified as the following types of infection: **lytic, chronic** (or continuous), and **latent** (or lysogenic).

Viruses that cause a lytic infection destroy the host cell to enable the progeny virus to escape and infect new target cells. Frequently, non-enveloped viruses (viruses with no host-derived lipid bilayer) are lytic because the cell's plasma membrane serves as a barrier for release. These viruses can, however, delay cell lysis, prolonging viral replication until very high numbers are obtained. Since death of the host cell immediately ensues upon release, viral progeny must be able to efficiently find and then infect new host cells. These may be neighboring cells or, if the virus is shed from the body, cells in an entirely different organism.

A chronic infection is started by viruses that can exit the cell without causing any damage such as cell lysis. Enveloped viruses, such as hantavirus, induce this type of infection. Instead of rupturing or lysing the cell, the virus simply buds off from the plasma or golgi membranes (Figure 3.1). This is thought to occur by interaction of some of the viral proteins to the bilipid layer of cellular membranes. Although cell lysis does not occur, cellular proliferation and normal protein synthesis can be delayed. Since viral mRNA sequesters cellular ribosomes—the site inside the host cell where protein synthesis occurs—the cell's production of protein can be slowed. As an analogy, imagine that you take the highway to get from your house to the beach, and imagine that this trip usually takes 10 minutes. Now imagine that it is a very hot day and everyone else wants to take the same highway to the beach. As a result, you are stuck in a traffic jam and the 10-minute trip lasts an hour. In the same way, the "highway" leading to protein production is now flooded with viral transcript, and the cell is delayed in its own functioning.

Latent infections result in a postponement of viral replication and release. Following infection, the virus simply exists within the cell in a dormant or inactive state, only replicating its own genome by incorporating it into the cell's DNA. In this way, the virus ensures that cellular propagation occurs and that future cells will be available to cause infection. One example of a virus that causes latent infection is the herpes virus. The initial herpes virus infection occurs in **neurons** (nerve cells). The virus does not replicate and thereby avoids attack by the host's immune system. When the host is subjected to a stressful stimulus (such as a physical injury), the virus takes this opportunity to "wake up" and start its replication cycle.

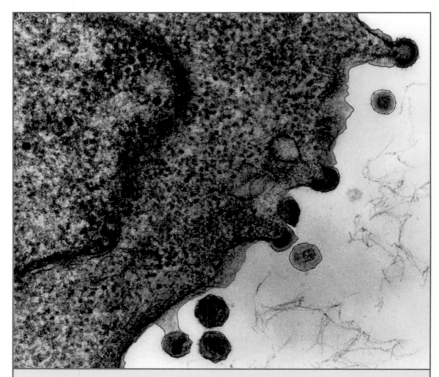

Figure 3.1 Viruses, such as hantavirus, obtain their lipid envelope by budding from the cell they infect. This lipid layer will also allow the virus to successfully infect another cell as the membranes fuse together.

The herpes virus then moves back down the axon of the neuron and quickly begins replication, which in turn leads to cellular damage and disease recurrence.

In addition to causing direct cellular damage, another important component of viral pathogenesis is the immune response. When a virus enters the host's body and cells, many signals are sent out to the immune system to indicate that a foreign invader is present. Cells can present viral antigens on their surface. These antigens are substances that serve as a flag to the immune system, making the infected cells easier for the immune cells to recognize and attack. Additionally, as a further defense mechanism, infected cells can make and release **cytokines** or **chemokines,** which are specialized chemicals that recruit white blood cells to the site of the viral infection. The result is that the immune response is activated and both innate and acquired immunity work to rid the body of the invading pathogen (see Chapter 4).

The processes described above are essential to the elimination of the virus and, ultimately, the survival of the host. These processes are not without risk to the host, however. The highly reactive cells of the immune system have an arsenal of proteins, enzymes, and chemical mediators that not only destroy the virus but may damage the host's cells in the process. Hantavirus infection and HPS are thought to provoke this type of overactive and prolonged immune response. In the process of trying to clear the infection in endothelial cells, lung capillaries become leaky and pulmonary edema results (Figure 3.2). Although hantavirus induces a chronic infection in cells and may induce cellular changes that affect cellular permeability, it does not directly lyse cells and therefore is not termed cytotoxic. The cellular damage that is observed in HPS is thought to be **immunopathologic,** meaning that it is a direct result of the immune response of the host.

HANTAVIRUS SPECIFICITY TOWARDS TISSUE TYPE

All viruses have specificity towards the type of cell they can infect due to their binding receptors. Think of this as a lock-and-key mechanism, where the virus presents a key that only opens the lock found on certain cells. For hantaviruses, the known receptors (the lock) to facilitate entry into the cell are known as the β_3 and β_1 integrins. The viral G1 and G2 proteins (the key) recognize these proteins and will stick to them. The integrins are adhesion molecules that are present on the cell surface and are differentially expressed depending on the cell type. The β_1 integrin is used by **nonpathogenic** hantaviruses (does not cause disease in humans), such as the Prospect Hill

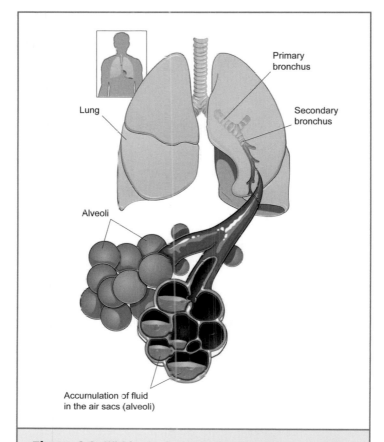

Figure 3.2 Within the lung are tiny air sacs, or alveoli, at the termini of bronchicles that normally allow for gas exchange. During the course of HPS, the alveoli are the sites of damage and subsequent pulmonary edema. Instead of air filling the alveoli, they become full of fluid.

strain. All of the **pathogenic** viruses (causing disease) use the β_3 integrin to gain entry into the cell. β_3 integrins are readily expressed on endothelial cells, where they are crucial for adhesion and regulating vascular permeability. They are also expressed on **platelets** (a type of cell required for blood clotting), where they regulate activation and adhesion. The β_3 integrin forms a functional complex with a partner α

chain protein. This pairing lends specificity for normal **ligand–receptor** interaction. Much as the viral proteins specifically recognize a certain integrin receptor, there are cellular ligands (like the keys in our example) that bind to the integrin

INTEGRINS

Integrins are cellular proteins that are expressed on the surface of the cell and are comprised of one alpha (α) and one beta (β) chain. The alpha and beta chain combinations have been found to interact to form at least 22 different receptor complexes all with different specificities for what they will bind and on what cell they may be expressed. They are critical for proper cell functioning as they contact other cells as well as fibrous proteins in their environment. Signals from these interactions have been shown to regulate such activities as cell growth, cell death, differentiation, and tumor cell migration. Integrins can be expressed on white blood cells that help them to migrate along blood vessels and enter into tissue where sites of infection are present. They may also be expressed on developing cells so they can receive the proper stimuli to help them fully mature. The $\alpha_v\beta_3$ integrin is widely expressed and is used in such processes as blood vessel growth and bone cell motility. This integrin can also be used in disease states as a means to promote tumor cell growth and increase the invasion of leukemias (cancer of the blood). While $\alpha_v\beta_3$ is a powerful receptor for both normal cell functioning and development, it can also be manipulated in the disease state. Integrins in general are attractive receptors for viral entry and $\alpha_v\beta_3$ is utilized by more than just the hantavirus. Other examples are the West Nile Virus, which is spread by mosquitoes and can cause severe or mild illness in humans, adenovirus that is responsible for respiratory disease uses $\alpha_v\beta_3$ as a co-receptor, and Foot and Mouth Disease caused by the coxsackievirus uses this integrin receptor.

for normal cellular functions. So if we consider these integrin receptors as a whole, there are many different combinations for α and β chains. For example, platelets are the only cell type to express $\alpha_{IIb}\beta_3$ and hantavirus can recognize this receptor. Another example is hantavirus recognition of the $\alpha_v\beta_3$ integrin, which is widely expressed on endothelial cells, muscle cells, bone cells (osteoclasts), and certain cells of the immune system. The fact that $\alpha_v\beta_3$ integrin is expressed on many cell types helps explain how the pathogenesis of hantavirus infection occurs. Once the virus has gained entry into the host and is deposited into the lung, the first stage of the immune response begins. Circulating macrophages (large cells of the immune system) that are always on the lookout for foreign entities and act to engulf (a process termed phagocytosis) any pathogen or foreign object, will most likely encounter the virus. Macrophages migrate or move along the endothelial cells that line blood vessels and ultimately squeeze between these cells into the tissue of the lung. Because these cells also express the receptor for hantavirus ($\alpha_v\beta_3$ integrin), they can become infected. Remember that hantavirus does not kill the cells that it infects, so the macrophage can continue moving about the lung. As this happens, the macrophage acts as a transport while the new virus is being made and released, and as new infections occur throughout the lung. It is also believed that macrophages carry the virus to more distant sites such as the kidney and other highly **vascularized** tissue. Taken together, hantavirus infection through the β_3 integrin complex primarily affects endothelial cells and platelets but may also affect other cells of the body. This leads to vessel leakage and poor blood clotting, which are the causes of pulmonary edema in HPS or hemorrhage and kidney failure in HFRS.

COMPARISON OF HPS AND HFRS

HPS and HFRS have many similarities. Even though they are derived from New and Old World viruses, respectively, they share a common pathogenesis. Both syndromes begin with inhalation of the virus, usually after it was shed from a rodent. Infection of endothelial cells of the respiratory tissues follows, which leads to changes in vascular permeability. The incubation phase for both types of hantavirus is 2 to 4 weeks and flu-like symptoms develop during this time or shortly thereafter. Where the course of each infection diverges is the

HERPES VIRUS

Herpes Simplex virus is the cause of cold sores (caused by HSV-1) as well as genital herpes (HSV-2). This virus infects primary neurons and begins a latent infection until such a time that it begins its replicative program. HSV-1 is the most common of the family of herpes viruses and transmission is through direct skin contact. Other herpes virus family members include varicella-zoster virus (causes chickenpox) and Epstein Barr Virus (causes mononucleosis). Once it has successfully entered into the neuron, the virus will travel up the length of the axon and will insert its DNA into the host cell's genome where it will remain dormant for quite some time and will not replicate. Upon some source of stress such as over exposure in the sun, a cold, or a run down immune system will cause the virus to begin its replication lifecycle. New virus particles are shed from the neuron and cellular damage is presented at the skin in the form of a sore or blister. Sometimes the immune system can clear certain herpes virus infections, other times, the virus is present for life. There is no cure, however, certain anti viral therapies can be used to keep the virus dormant and prevent outbreaks. Herpes viruses of different species can infect other mammals as well and one such host is the cat. These infections cause respiratory problems as well as secondary outbreaks in the eye and around the mucous membranes of the mouth. Again, there is no cure but some anti viral therapies are available.

target organ. In HPS, the lung is primarily affected and pulmonary edema is the main cause of death. There is little or no renal involvement, although endothelial cells in the kidney have been shown to be infected in some cases. HFRS causes hemorrhages of capillaries and may be apparent as flushing of the face or blood in the eye. This is further extended to the kidney, where renal failure may eventually occur. Patients who survive HPS and HFRS may take weeks or months to fully recover from the infection and tissue damage. HPS has a higher mortality rate (36%) than HFRS (7%).

4

The Immune Response: Our First Line of Defense Against Viruses

Microorganisms and infectious agents are all around us. Without our knowledge, our bodies serve as a battleground between bacteria, viruses, other pathogens, and the white blood cells of our immune system. The immune system is the first line of defense against any foreign pathogen, and we are constantly encountering them. Many common daily activities put us into contact with bacteria and viruses. Using a public telephone, gardening in our yard, and even opening a door can bring pathogens on and into our bodies. Most of the time, our immune system can recognize and neutralize these organisms before they have had time to replicate—and before we were ever even aware of their presence. Other times, the virus or bacterium is quite infectious and is able to sneak past immune surveillance for a time. Ultimately, however, the immune system comes into action to battle and hopefully eliminate the pathogen. The immune response can be categorized into multiple components such as physical barriers (our skin and mucous membranes), chemical mediators that call white blood cells into action, and each of the immune system's specialized cells (for example, phagocytes and lymphocytes). Collectively, these components help to keep us healthy and fight against any infectious agent that has managed to invade our bodies (Figure 4.1).

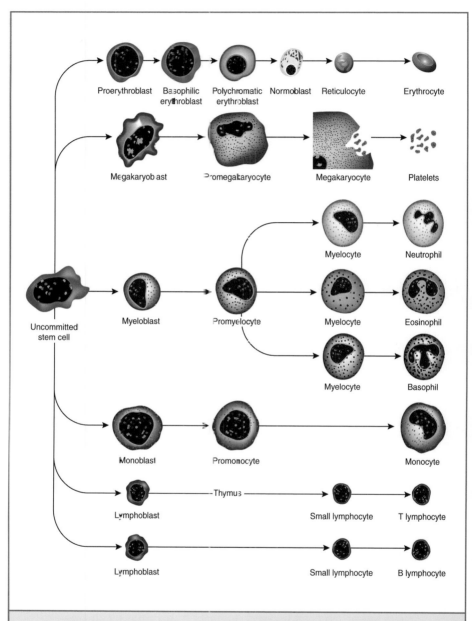

Figure 4.1 The differentiation of both red and white blood cells requires many steps that all originate from a single stem cell.

OVERVIEW OF THE IMMUNE SYSTEM

There are two arms of the immune system: **innate** and **acquired** immunity. Innate immunity accounts for the defense mechanisms that are present from the time of birth. These include the skin, mucous membranes (such as those lining the nasal passages), **proteases** (enzymes that destroy protein), circulating molecules (such as a component called complement) and a family of white blood cells known as leukocytes. These components of immunity are always present and respond to all types of foreign invaders, from infectious biological entities to foreign bodies such as splinters. The two most important of the innate immune cells are the neutrophils and macrophages,

NEUTROPHILS

Neutrophils or polymorphonuclear leukocytes are the most abundant of all the white blood cells (about 70% of all white blood cells). As an adult, humans produce billions every day. Although neutrophils are primarily known for their amazing ability to eat and destroy bacteria, they are involved in all facets of inflammation. They are the first responders to any sight of infection as their large population size always ensures that one or more is nearby. Neutrophils will react to foreign objects such as slivers of wood or metal embedded in the skin, as well as viruses, bacteria, fungi, and yeast. So what makes neutrophils so good at what they do? Inside each of these power houses of immunity lies specialized granules filled with highly reactive and highly toxic chemicals and proteases. Upon interaction with a foreign body, the neutrophil will release this arsenal of chemicals in hopes of neutralizing or killing the infectious agent, and if that isn't enough, it will then clean up the mess it made by phagocytosing the pathogen. These leukocytes only live for about one day before undergoing a although other cells such as eosinophils and basophils also play a role. Neutrophils and macrophages are highly reactive against any foreign pathogen, and they have but one goal: seek and destroy. These immune cells release a barrage of enzymes and other chemicals to destroy the invading pathogen and then finish the job by cleaning up the resulting debris. In addition to fighting viral infections, these calls are particularly good at eating bacteria and even clearing an area of dead or dying cells. Another important phagocyte closely involved in fighting viral infections is the natural killer (NK) cell. These white blood cells recognize virally infected cells and target them for destruction so that the virus cannot propagate.

highly structured cell death process called apoptosis. This type of cell death is very important for this cell as it ensures that all of the toxic reagents it carries inside will not simply leak out into the normal cellular environment. If that were to happen, these chemicals and proteases would also damage healthy cells and would lead to further recruitment of white blood cells in a process known as inflammation. Inflammation is characterized as an acute or rapid immune response. A classic example of this is what happens when bacteria on the surface of your skin gets into underlying tissue, as the result of a cut. The site of the cut becomes red, swollen, and painful to the touch but within a day or two things feel better, and the cut is healing as if nothing ever happened. Neutrophils are immediately alerted to the problem, as they arrive in massive numbers and destroy all bacteria. Once the infectious agent is gone, neutrophils die off and healing begins. We depend on this process and this cell type to fend off numerous pathogens on a daily basis.

Acquired or specific immunity involves the family of white blood cells known as the lymphocytes. This type of immunity is activated in response to a very specific foreign **antigen**. An antigen is the part of the pathogen that the immune system recognizes as "non-self." Antigens activate both T- and B-lymphocytes. As an analogy, the antigen is the virus's "business card." It contains all the information needed for the immune system to recognize it and respond accordingly. T-lymphocytes are involved in cell mediated immunity, which means that they either further activate the immune response or lyse virally infected cells. B-lymphocytes are involved in **humoral immunity**, which is the production of **antibodies** against a specific antigen. Once these antibodies have been made and secreted by B-lymphocytes, one of two things can happen next. One, the antibody can directly bind to the virus itself (known as a neutralizing antibody) and render it unable to bind to its host receptor. In this way, the virus is stopped from infecting new cells. The other possibility is that the antibody can bind to the virally infected cell and act as a "red-flag" to target these cells for destruction by white blood cells.

Assume that a virus has successfully made it past all physical barriers and has reached the lung. It infects a target cell and begins to replicate. Leukocytes of the innate immune system are constantly moving throughout the body. They come across a stray virus, and thus the battle begins. Phagocytes try and clear the virus but viral propagation has already led to hundreds if not thousands of viral progeny very quickly. More phagocytes are recruited to the area to try and contain the infection, but at the same time the acquired immune response has been activated and lymphocytes are drawn into the fight as well. Large populations of B- and T-lymphocytes (also known as B- and T-cells) that recognize the virus grow rapidly and increased antibody production leads to viral neutralization as infected cells are destroyed. This collective process continues until the virus has been eliminated, after which healing of tissues can begin. What we are then left with is known as **immunologic memory**, which means that if the virus ever enters the body again, the immune system will immediately recognize and quickly destroy it before any symptoms of disease can occur.

IMMUNE RESPONSE TO VIRAL INFECTIONS

If we examine the immune response to viruses more closely, we can begin to understand the cellular mechanisms that occur. It becomes clear that there is an interaction between T- and B- lymphocytes, and that this interaction between them fully activates the anti-viral attack. As stated previously, B-lymphocytes make antibodies that specifically recognize viral antigens. The first type of antibody that is made is known as immunoglobulin M (IgM). The antibody is not released from the lymphocyte but instead remains bound and localized on the cell membrane. Once the IgM antibody comes in contact with a virus, it becomes tightly bound to the virus. When this happens, the virus-bound IgM complex is internalized and "chewed up" by the B-lymphocyte. This process occurs so that one or more of the resulting tiny viral fragments can be displayed on the surface of the B-lymphocyte, thus enabling it to be seen by a T-lymphocyte. To use our analogy again, it is as if the B-lymphocyte is showing the viral business card to the T-lymphocyte. This method of communication between the B- and T-lymphocytes results in a massive expansion in the number of B-cells, which is followed by the production of secreted IgM (Figure 4.2).

Another class of antibody that is produced is immunoglobulin G (IgG). This antibody is the major form found in serum and can activate the complement cascade, which comprises 20 serum proteins that, when activated, link together on a virally infected cell. This process forms channels (pokes holes) in the plasma membrane and causes the cell

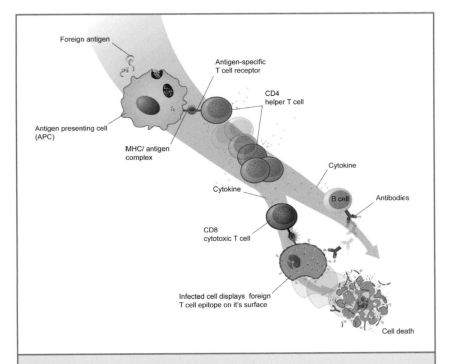

Figure 4.2 Both T- and B- lymphocytes must work together to recognize and destroy viruses and virally infected cells. Using a series of cell surface recognition molecules, T-cells are alerted to the presence of a virus, and B-cells begin to produce specific antibodies to neutralize viruses and prevent further infection.

to lyse. B-cells are very important for antibody production, as they mediate viral neutralization and clearance.

T-lymphocytes can be further divided into two groups: helper T-cells (also referred to as CD4+) and cytotoxic T-cells (CD8+). The "cluster of differentiation" (CD) system is a system of naming cell surface proteins that is used to identify the lineage of the cell. The CD4 receptor (T-helper cell) binds to another protein on macrophages or B-cells called the MHC II (major histocompatibility complex) molecule. The MHC II complex also can present a viral antigen to a T-cell to increase the immune response. In this way, the T-helper cell is alerted to the presence of a virus and begins to make a variety of chemical and protein mediators to recruit more white blood cells into the battle against the pathogen. The cytotoxic T-cell's CD8 receptor binds to a slightly different complex known as the MHC I molecule, which also presents viral antigen. The difference is that MHC I expression and viral presentation is on a virally infected cell. If the attention of a cytotoxic T-cell is brought to a virally infected cell, the result will be the death of the cell and all viral progeny. Simply stated, T-helper cells strengthen the anti viral response by directing other immune cells and cytotoxic T-cells to kill virally infected cells.

In addition to cell-to-cell activation of white blood cells, there is a multitude of signaling molecules that act in the anti viral response. These mediators are collectively referred to as cytokines and chemokines. While both classes are small proteins and affect the behavior of cells, chemokines are specific in that they cause the movement of white blood cells into the site of infection. One class of cytokine that is very important against viral infection is the interferons (IFNs). Interferons inhibit viral replication by turning off protein synthesis inside a cell. They are also able to stimulate antibody production by B-lymphocytes. Another cytokine, tumor necrosis factor-alpha (TNF-α), activates numerous cells of the immune system and can even induce cell death. There are many members of the interleukin (IL) family of cytokines, but IL-12 further stimulates IFN production and IL-10 induces B-lymphocyte growth. Taken together, the immune response is a complex network of cellular contacts and soluble mediators. This system of synchronized interactions and responses not only allows for efficient viral clearance, but also holds a "cellular memory" in case the pathogen returns.

IMMUNE RESPONSE TO HANTAVIRUS

Samples taken from patients infected with the Sin Nombre virus have been used to study the humoral and cellular

HIV

Human Immunodeficiency Virus or HIV is the virus that causes AIDS (Acquired Immune Deficiency Syndrome). This virus is known as a retrovirus, which means that is has two (+) strands of RNA that are converted to DNA by an enzyme called reverse transcriptase. Once the DNA version of its genome has been made, it can insert itself into the host genome and cause a latent infection. Although there may be mild nondescript symptoms (fever, aches, and pains) after infection, the virus does not induce any other symptoms for many years. During this period, the virus can easily be transmitted to other humans through blood or intimate contact with an infected person. So if the immune system does such a great job of recognizing and eventually eliminating viral pathogens, why should HIV be any different? The key to HIV is that it infects and destroys the very cells that are needed to mount an effective immune response. HIV targets the CD4 receptor that is on CD4+ T-helper cells and macrophages. Therefore, HIV infects the T-helper lymphocytes and turns them into a viral production factory. Slowly, the HIV virus will cause T-cell numbers to decrease. That is the point at which the person is diagnosed with AIDS. Since an arm of the immune response has been effectively knocked out or severely attenuated, it becomes difficult to fight off any foreign pathogen, even the common cold. The person may die from various opportunistic infections simply because the immune system cannot work properly. There are treatments that can slow down viral replication and prevent further infection, but there is no cure. HIV infection and AIDS is a global problem. It is estimated that approximately 40 million people worldwide are infected.

responses in HPS. The main antigens for antibody production have been the nucleocapsid protein (N) as well as glycoproteins G1 and G2. All HPS patients tested had IgM production against the N antigen at the start of clinical symptoms. Additionally, almost all those infected with SNV also showed IgG production to N and G1 antigens. The normal course of antibody production in mild cases of HPS where the patient fully recovered started with IgM and then rapidly progressed to IgG production. Additionally, there was a strong presence of neutralizing antibodies. In contrast, patients with the most severe clinical course of infection had low levels of IgG and neutralizing antibodies. During the recovery phase, the highest titers (levels) of IgG were seen within two weeks and lasted for months.

The cellular response to hantavirus is characterized by a large growth of the population of CD8+ cytotoxic T-lymphocytes. These cells are of utmost importance for viral clearance and are also thought to correlate with the severity of the disease. Since cytotoxic T-cells lyse virally infected cells, it is believed that these cells will destroy infected endothelial cells, thereby weakening the overall vascular architecture. This causes vascular permeability and accounts for fluid accumulation within the lung. Early in the course of infection, increases in neutrophils, monocytes, B-cells, and T-cells are observed. There is also an increase in circulating immunoblasts, which in the case of HPS primarily gives rise to CD4+ and CD8+ T-lymphocytes. NK cell involvement has not been well characterized; however, an overall drop in circulating NK cells has been observed and may indicate migration into the lung tissue early in disease.

Cytokine production during hantavirus infection is a major cause of HPS symptoms. TNF-α, IL-1, and IL-6 are **pyrogenic,** which means that they have the ability to induce a fever. TNF-α is a very potent pro-inflammatory cytokine and can result in a large infiltration of leukocytes into the lung. The continual production of TNF-α has also been shown to play a role in vascular leakage. When hantavirus-infected endothelial cells are exposed to TNF-α, they become irreversibly hyper-permeable and allow fluid and blood leakage into the lung. Collectively, the immune response is critical for viral clearance but in the process it may also be responsible for cellular damage to the lung that leads to pulmonary edema. If antibodies are produced quickly and in high titers, it appears that the course of the disease is milder. Since the immune system's cellular response is so powerful (and it has to be to fend off daily pathogen attacks), the key to the resolution of the disease is a delicate balance between viral and cellular destruction and a rapid downregulation of the immune response once the virus has been contained. Clinical studies indicate that a rapid neutralization of the virus that is mediated by antibodies leads to a shorter and milder course of disease followed by a speedy recovery.

5

Viral Transmission

Although hantavirus infections in the Americas are rare, it is important to understand how the virus is spread. The route of transmission is directly from a rodent source to a human. The virus is shed in the saliva, urine, or feces of the rodent and can readily become airborne. Hantavirus can remain infectious for many days in a natural setting, although direct sunlight can shorten this period Since the virus has a lipid envelope, it is also inactivated when exposed to detergents that are present in many cleaning agents. The many species of hantavirus that cause HPS are only carried by certain rodents, but collectively the natural habitats of these rodents encompass most of North and South America.

RODENT RESERVOIRS

The majority of Bunyaviridae viruses are transmitted to humans through insect bites. Hantaviruses are an exception in that they are only transmitted by infected rodents. Although the hantaviruses responsible for HPS must first infect the rodent carrier, they do not cause any significant or obvious illness in them. There are four rodents in the United States that have been shown to carry the New World hantaviruses: the deer mouse (*Peromyscus maniculatus*), the white-footed mouse (*Peromyscus leucopus*) (Figure 5.1a), the cotton rat (*Sigmodon hispidus*) (Figure 5.1b), and the rice rat (*Oryzomys palustris*). It should be noted, however, that other rodent species could also carry these viruses. There are at least 430 similar species of rodents throughout North and South America.

The deer mouse is responsible for the majority of HPS infections in the United States. It is the host for the Sin Nombre virus (SNV) and its habitat is widespread throughout rural areas in the United States, including

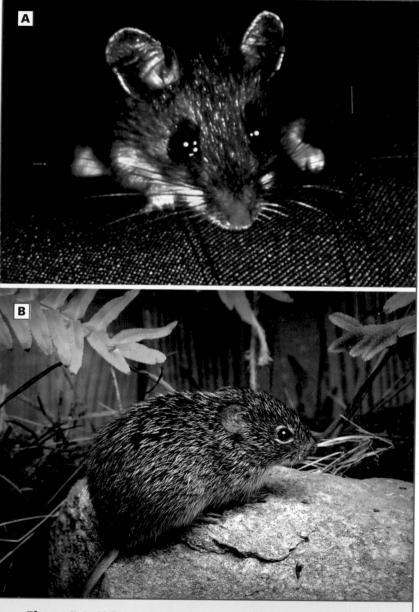

Figure 5.1 A) The white-footed mouse (*Peromyscus leucopus*) and B) The cotton rat (*Sigmodon hispidus*) are two rodent species known to carry different strains of hantavirus causing HPS.

woodlands and deserts. The deer mouse has also been found in urban and suburban areas which increases the risk for human contact. Characteristics include large eyes and ears, a body 2 to 3 inches in length plus a tail that is also 2 to 3 inches long, coloring from gray to reddish brown, and a white underbelly. It is believed that, on average, 10% of the deer mouse population has been infected with SNV, although this number is significantly higher in certain regions of the country.

The white-footed mouse is the carrier of the New York virus and is associated with both suburban and rural environments. Its habitat in the United States ranges from southern New England and the Mid-Atlantic states to the Midwest and Mexico. Although its appearance resembles that of the deer mouse, there are a couple of differences. The tail of the white-footed mouse is shorter than its body, the color of the fur is pale to reddish brown, and its underbelly and feet are white.

The next two hantavirus reservoirs are rats that are generally only found in rural areas among shrubs and tall grasses. The cotton rat, a carrier of the Black Creek Canal virus, is found in the southeastern United States as well as in Central and South America. It is approximately 5 to 7 inches long with a tail length of 3 inches. Its fur is long, course, and grayish-brown. The rice rat, the carrier of the Bayou virus, is smaller than the cotton rat but has a very long tail (4 to 7 inches). Similar to the cotton rat, its habitat is the southeastern United States and central America and it can be found in marshes as it is partially aquatic. Two additional rodent species, the brush mouse (*Peromyscus boylii*) and the Western harvest mouse (*Reithrodontomys megalotis*), have been associated with hantaviruses but no human disease has yet been reported from them.

TRANSMISSION TO HUMANS
Direct rodent handling by a human does not have to occur for viral transmission to occur. The most common method for

viral transmission is through the release of tiny aerosolized droplets from fresh urine, saliva, or droppings (Figure 5.2). Since the virus remains infectious for several days, dried excreta may also become airborne and thus be inhaled. Less common routes of transmission include a direct bite from a rodent, touching a contaminated object and then touching the nose or mouth, or eating food contaminated with rodent excreta. These uncommon routes of transmission are more likely to occur if there is either direct handling of the rodent or if rodents invade food stores by gnawing through boxes or sacs. Hantaviruses are not carried by arthropods such as fleas, ticks, or mosquitoes, nor are they known to infect livestock such as cows, chicken, or sheep. Humans cannot contract hantavirus from common pet store animals such as guinea pigs, hamsters, or gerbils, and since only specific species carry the virus, rodents sold in pet stores are safe as well. Cats and dogs do not carry or transfer hantavirus, although they may bring rodents in closer proximity to the home. One should therefore be aware of any dead rodents brought to the front doorstep by a pet and should take the proper cleanup precautions.

TRANSMISSION BY HUMANS

One puzzling aspect of HPS when it was first described was that it was infrequent to see multiple members of the same household infected with the virus. We now understand that the hantavirus strains present in the United States cannot be transmitted between humans. This is further evidenced by the fact that no health care worker, while caring for an HPS patient, has ever been infected with the virus. Additionally, hantavirus cannot be transmitted by touching, hugging, or kissing an infected person. It is also known that blood transfusions are safe using blood from individuals that contracted HPS and fully recovered. Although none of the North American hantavirus species have been shown to be transmitted between humans, this is not so for South American hantavirus species. In the spring of

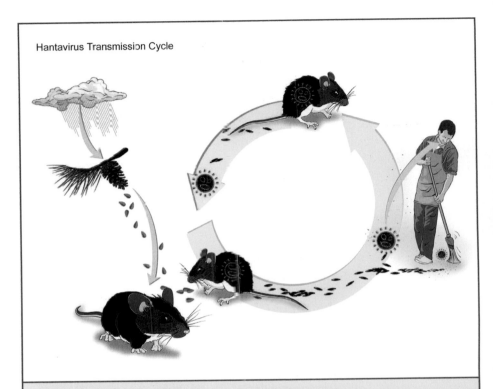

Hantavirus Transmission Cycle

Figure 5.2 Environmental factors influence the transmission of hantavirus. Upon heavy rainfall and abundant plant growth, the rodent populations expand. This expansion puts humans at an increased risk of coming into contact with rodent droppings and aerosolized hantavirus.

1996, an outbreak of HPS caused by the Andes virus occurred in southern Argentina. In this outbreak, person-to-person transmission was well documented. In another HPS outbreak of 25 cases in southern Chile between July 1997 and January 1998, human transmission was strongly suspected, as family members having no contact with rodents became infected with the Andes virus. Whether this viral property of human-to-human transmission has always been species-specific or is the result of genetic change within the New World hantaviruses is unknown.

COULD HANTAVIRUSES BE USED AS A BIOWEAPON?

In recent years, there has been an elevated threat of the possibility of bioterrorism. News reports have been flooded with anthrax scares and the renewal of smallpox vaccinations. Since HPS is an infectious disease with relatively high fatality, it raises the question as to whether hantaviruses could be used in biological warfare. To answer this question it is helpful to first consider the properties of a bioweapon: It must be possible to

SMALLPOX

Smallpox has resurfaced as a potential virus to be used for bioterrorism. It is caused by the variola virus and was effectively eradicated by vaccination programs. This vaccine program was stopped in the 1970s as the last natural outbreak was reported in 1977. The virus does still exist in laboratories where research is being done. Transmission of the virus occurs by direct and prolonged human contact. Additionally, this virus may be spread from body fluids or any clothing or bedding that has been infected. Following infection, there is an incubation period usually ranging between 12-14 days where the person is not infectious. Next is the prodrome phase with fever, body aches, and general malaise. As the disease progresses and the person becomes contagious, a rash of small red spots develops in the mouth which become sores and break open. A rash will then develop on the skin and spread to all parts of the body. This rash develops into bumps, then pustules that will eventually scab over and fall off within three weeks after the rash first appears. Those that survive this infection will be left with pitted scars where the sores had formed. The United States government currently has enough vaccine for every person if an outbreak were to occur. Although there is no effective treatment, new drugs are being studied for their anti viral properties toward the variola virus.

produce in extremely large quantities while maintaining its stability. Additionally, the candidate infectious agent must be airborne, easily transmissible produce high fatality rates, and have a low infectious dose. When examining these properties it becomes clear that naturally occurring hantavirus strains would not be amenable to development as a bioweapon.

ANTHRAX

Anthrax is an infectious disease that is caused by the bacterium *Bacillus anthracis*. The bacterium enters a stage of its lifecycle where it forms a dormant spore and becomes resistant to the environment. Once it enters into a host, it can begin growing again. This disease can be spread to humans as well as to cattle, sheep, and goats. Anthrax can occur as a cutaneous (skin), inhaled, or gastrointestina infection, although the most common is through a cut in the skin. The site where the bacterial spore enters will result in an itchy bump that will then turn into an ulcer. If the bacteria are allowed to progress unchecked, they may enter into the bloodstream and the patient would become septic. Cutaneous infections, if left untreated, are fatal in about 20% of the cases. Anthrax infections respond well to antimicrobial medication such as Ciproxin. If, however, the bacterium is inhaled, the disease will progress to severe breathing problems and is usually fatal. Gastrointestinal anthrax infection occurs when infected meat is eaten. Nausea, vomiting, fever, and abdominal pain are the symptoms and fatality rates range from 25 - 60%. The danger from anthrax infection not only lies with the replicating bacteria, but also with the toxic substance that they produce. Anthrax cannot be transmitted between people and in addition to antibiotics, a vaccine has also been developed with a 93% efficiency to protect from infection. Every year the natural incidence of anthrax infections are low with only one to two cases reported.

Hantavirus isolation and growth in cell culture has been extremely difficult and requires specialized equipment, training, reagents, and housing. Although it is airborne, only the Andes virus has been shown to spread through human contact. The New World viruses are much more **virulent** than the Old World hantaviruses, but even so, fatality rates are dropping due to medical intervention and early diagnosis. Hantaviruses are stable for days in the environment, however direct sunlight and detergents such as those in hand soap will inactivate them. In fact, the CDC has designed a category system to classify biological agents as potential bioweapons. Category A represents the greatest threat for bioweapon development and includes such infectious particles as anthrax and smallpox. Category B describes agents that can cause moderate disease and are relatively easy to distribute. Hantavirus is classified as category C, which represents emerging infectious diseases that may be engineered as a biological weapon. The viruses in this category are a minimal risk, as they require extensive genetic manipulation to become a large-scale threat. Taken together, the hantaviruses that cause HPS do not currently pose a threat for bioweapon development.

6

Clinical Presentation and Treatment

You recently spent the weekend cleaning out your garage, removing clutter and stirring up dust. While removing several storage boxes, you see what looks like a rodent nest with bits of shredded paper and cotton fiber. A sudden movement catches your attention as you see a gray mouse run out through a small hole in your garage wall. You notice that the floor is littered with droppings. After cleaning up the mess, you put out several rodent traps and go about your normal routine. Two weeks later, you suddenly develop flu-like symptoms and you remember your rodent encounter. What should you do if hantavirus infection is suspected? What are the symptoms?

SYMPTOMS

Once one of the hantavirus species that causes HPS has been inhaled, it settles in the lungs and can take 1 to 3 weeks before any clinical symptoms arise. The virus can be aerosolized from rodent saliva or excreta, or in very rare cases the virus can be transmitted by rodent bites, ingestion of virally tainted food, or through broken skin. In general, symptoms can be classified into early and late stages (Figure 6.1). The early stage can last 3 to 5 days, and is generally characterized by flu-like symptoms including sudden fever, body aches, headache, nausea, and vomiting. During this phase, respiratory problems, cough, and sore throat are not evident. Physical exams and chest X-rays appear normal during this time. After this **febrile** or **prodromal** phase, the late-stage and life-threatening symptoms begin quite abruptly. **Cardiopulmonary** involvement becomes evident from difficulty in breathing; this

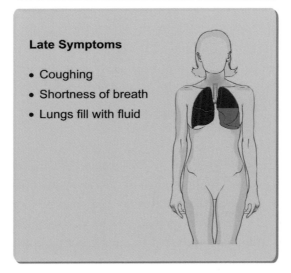

Figure 6.1 The early symptoms of HPS can last a few days and include fever, dizziness, aches, chills, and nausea. Late symptoms, including coughing and shortness of breath, occur after one week of infection and evolve quickly. Patients usually become hospitalized at the late stage.

is the time at which most patients are hospitalized. Depending on the severity of the symptoms, supplemental oxygen may be given or mechanical ventilation may be necessary. At this stage the lungs fill with fluid **(edema),** resulting in shortness of breath, coughing, and rapid heartbeat. In the most severe cases,

ANTIBODIES

An antibody is a specialized "Y" shaped protein called an immunoglobulin that is comprised of four chains known as the heavy and light chains (size and molecular weight). Antibodies are specifically produced by B-lymphocytes in response to an antigen present within the body. The "Y" complex is made of two heavy chains and two light chains. This complex can also be divided into the variable region (the part that identifies and binds to the specific antigen) and the constant region (the "backbone" of the complex). Antibodies can be put into subcategories known as IgG, IgM, IgA, IgD, and IgE and are classified as such depending on the type of heavy chain, as well as if there are multiple antibodies linked together such as IgM. Besides their important role in immune mediated responses, antibodies have become powerful biological tools in research. Antibodies can be modified so that they are fluorescently tagged or so their presence will show a color change or an emission of light. Using these principles, antibodies can be used to detect a specific protein that can then be visualized by the scientist. Antibodies as cellular tools can help to answer such questions as when and where is a specific protein expressed in an experimental setting. As an example, let's say we wanted to ask the question, "What is the cellular localization of the $\alpha_v\beta_3$ receptor before and after hantavirus infection?" We could answer that question by collecting and staining cells with antibodies against the $\alpha_v\beta_3$ receptor. With the use of a fluorescent tag and a microscope, we could see how the receptor moves by the pattern of fluorescence.

very low blood pressure **(hypotension)** and an abnormal heart-beat **(arrhythmia)** are observed.

DIAGNOSIS

There are many clinical tests that can quickly indicate the likelihood of hantavirus infection. Additionally, more specialized tests are now available to give an absolute diagnosis. Once admitted to the hospital, the patient's blood is drawn and multiple parameters are examined in a test called a complete blood count (CBC). Since the initial symptoms of hantavirus infection are similar to those of other infectious agents (such as the influenza virus or pneumococcal bacteria), blood test results must be closely scrutinized. One of the earliest indicators of HPS is a low **platelet** count, also known as **thrombocytopenia**. Platelets are required for blood clotting, so it is no surprise that HPS patients display an increase in clotting times. White blood cell counts indicate an elevation in the overall number of these cells **(leukocytosis),** with a particular increase in the formation of immature **neutrophils**. Neutrophils are the most numerous of all the white blood cells and serve to defend the body from a variety of foreign pathogens. In hantavirus infection, the bone marrow (which produces white blood cells) is overactive as it tries to rapidly increase the total number of neutrophils. A third white blood cell indicator of HPS is the presence of circulating **immunoblasts,** which are large atypical T-lymphocytes. These cells mature to become different types of T-cells.

Specialized tests are used for a positive identification of the presence of the virus. One test used is the enzyme-linked immunosorbent assay (ELISA), in which a viral antigen (such as the viral nucleocapsid protein of the G1 glycoprotein) is deposited into an assay plate, mixed with serum extracted from patient blood, and incubated. If the patient is making antibodies to the viral antigen (which indicates infection with hantavirus), these patient-derived antibodies bind tightly to the viral protein in the assay plate. Through subsequent steps, one can see by a color change if the antibody is present. This test is simple to read, as the development of color indicates the presence of hantavirus infection. Since hantavirus proteins are similar between species, it is possible to use this test to detect many strains of hantavirus. Another test that can be performed is known as reverse transcription polymerase chain reaction (RT-PCR). This method is used to amplify viral RNA using specific primers that only recognize viral nucleic acid. This test indicates that there is a current, active viral infection.

ELISA

ELISA or Enzyme Linked Immunosorbent Assay, is a useful laboratory and clinical technique. ELISA is used in medicine to determine if a patient has been infected with a certain pathogen. The principal of the technique is that an antigen is deposited onto an ELISA plate that is made up of many tiny wells. Each antigen is very specific for the pathogen such as hantavirus or HIV. Serum from the patient's blood is added into the well coated with the antigen. If antibodies to that antigen are present from the patient sample, they will bind tightly in the assay well. From this point, there has to be a way to detect the presence of the patient's antibody and to do this, another (secondary) antibody is used. This secondary antibody is special for two reasons: 1. It will recognize any human antibody to any foreign pathogen and 2. This secondary antibody has been modified so that an enzyme is associated with it. This enzyme, when given a specific substrate, will cleave it and produce a color change. The color change happens only if the secondary antibody is present. The secondary antibody is present only if a patient antibody is present on the bound antigen, and patients only produce antibodies if the viral infection is present. Therefore, a color change means the patient has been infected with the specific pathogen for which the test was designed.

Direct isolation and propagation of the virus from an infected patient has been problematic, as hantavirus grows poorly once removed from its host. Postmortem tests reveal severe edema of the lungs without any direct viral damage to the cells they infected. This means that the virus was not **cytopathic** and did not cause the cells to die or break open. The virus does, however, activate the immune response. Due to viral localization in endothelial cells, the virus causes excessive immune-mediated damage in the lung, which leads to vessel leakage and pulmonary edema. Tissue samples stained for viral antigens indicate endothelial cell infection in the lungs, kidneys, heart, pancreas, adrenal glands, and skeletal muscle. Although Old World hantaviruses that cause HFRS primarily affect the kidney, HPS shows little or no renal involvement or hemorrhage.

COURSE OF INFECTION

After the virus has incubated and clinical symptoms become apparent, there are five distinct phases during the course of infection. The first is the febrile phase, in which flu-like symptoms begin and continue for about five days. The second (hypotensive) phase begins abruptly around day five, as the patient's symptoms become more severe. A drop in blood pressure is observed and edema is seen on X-ray examination (Figure 6.2). The next phase is called the oliguric phase, in which capillary leakage increases rapidly, and cardiac involvement is apparent. This is considered a critical stage for the patient. Either recovery will begin by a rapid progression into stage four or the patient will die. In stage four (the diuretic phase) the body begins to eliminate excess fluid by creating urine. Stage five is a prolonged **convalescence**, during which the body must fully recover and heal from the viral infection. Normal lung function usually returns, though this may take weeks to months of rest.

Although mortality from HPS has dropped from nearly 70% in 1993 when it was first identified to 36% as of 2005,

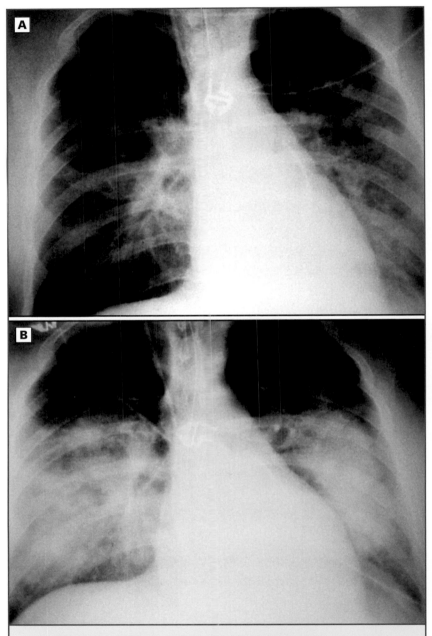

Figure 6.2 Chest X-rays from A) a normal patient and B) a patient with HPS where fluid is accumulating within the lungs.

there is a high variability in the outcome of the infection. Early treatment and admission to the hospital before pulmonary symptoms begin help to improve survival, but several other factors influence viral pathogenicity. One variable is simply the genetics of the patient. The general immune response, the rate of tissue regeneration, and the expression of viral receptors also influence viral burden. The amount of virus (the **inoculum** size of inhaled virus) can alter the course of infection, as can the specific viral species.

TREATMENT AND VACCINATION

If HPS is suspected, there are several measures that clinicians can take. Since pulmonary edema is the major risk factor, the patient must be given oxygen, by mechanical ventilation if necessary. Excess hydration should be avoided, as fluid leakage in the lungs impedes the ability to breathe. As of late 2004, the Food and Drug Administration (FDA) has not approved any antiviral or immunotherapeutic drug therapy that is specific for HPS. There have been, however, preliminary studies and proposals for the following therapies:

- Ribavirin: A **guanosine** analogue designed to inhibit viral replication. In 1991, scientists found that patients with HFRS had a sevenfold decrease in mortality when ribavirin was administered intravenously. Unfortunately, it did not show promising results for patients with HPS already presenting with cardiopulmonary symptoms.

- Studies by scientists utilized a system of Hantaan virus infection in mice. They demonstrated that pretreatment with the cytokine IFN-β (interferon beta) dramatically increased survival by up to 90%.

- Since the patients' own immune system causes the cellular damage leading to pulmonary edema, the use of steroids or cytokine antagonists to suppress the immune response may be an option. Additionally, the use of antibodies to block the β_3 integrin might prevent viral attachment, cellular entry, and therefore viral spread.

- Recently, scientists have identified peptides that are able to prevent Sin Nombre virus and Hantaan virus infection through β_3 integrins in cells. These experiments were conducted in tissue culture and pose an interesting therapeutic potential to inhibit further viral infection.

- Recently, the first animal model of HPS has been described, as the Andes virus is capable of causing HPS in hamsters. This allows for the study of the virus and its pathogenesis, and the design of effective treatments.

Another line of defense against HPS even before viral infection would be the design of an effective vaccine. A commercially available vaccine from Korea named Hantavax™ has been used for 10 years and is quite safe. The basis for the vaccination is an intact but inactive Hantaan virus that must be administered three times. Although trials have shown that the vaccine protects both humans and mice from disease, only 50% of humans respond by producing neutralizing antibodies to the virus. To increase an overall higher effective immunity, it may be possible to use one or more viral proteins as an **immunogen** for vaccination. Future work should be directed towards a safe and efficacious vaccine design for HPS.

7

Epidemiology of Hantaviruses

Whenever there is an increase in contact between humans and rodents, their habitat, or their excreta, the risk of hantavirus exposure also increases. Such contact can occur by recreational or occupational exposures or may be due to a surge in the population of rodents brought about by changes in the climate. Simply stated, if the overall number of rodents rises, the likelihood that their territory will expand into human dwellings becomes a greater risk. Although the chance of contracting a hantavirus in North America is low (20 to 50 cases per year since 1993), it is important to understand the **epidemiology** of this disease.

WHO IS AT RISK FOR HANTAVIRUS INFECTION?

The greatest single risk for exposure to hantavirus is working, playing, or living in an area of rodent infestation. The risk is greater during seasons where outdoor activity increases, such as spring and summer, which explains why more cases of HPS are seen during these times. Certain activities also increase the chance for becoming exposed to the virus. These activities include planting or harvesting crops, occupying a summer cabin that has been vacant, cleaning out storage sheds or barns, and hiking or camping. Although the deer mouse may be viewed as a cute and desirable pet, one should never touch, handle, or bring home a wild rodent. Cleaning one's home or yard can also increase the risk of exposure, as rodent dens or excreta may be encountered. In this case, however, taking proper precautions—such as wetting down the infected area with a 10% bleach solution or a detergent-based disinfectant—decreases the chance of transmission if the virus is indeed present.

Occupational exposure carries the highest risk, as there is either a continual exposure to rodents or a known interaction with the virus. Laboratory scientists actively working with strains of hantavirus must implement a system of universal precautions and use respirators and enclosed chambers with filtered ventilation. A properly equipped laboratory can ensure that the scientist does not risk viral exposure. Since these professionals work directly with the culture and manipulation of the live virus, they require the highest level of biosafety precautions to prevent accidental exposure. Those working in the field (such as field biologists) are at high risk for exposure, as they must enter rodent habitats. In the field, there are no chambers or regulated ventilation systems, so extreme caution must be taken when trapping rodents and studying their habitat. In fact, when field biologists and rodent workers were tested for antibodies to SNV, 1.14% turned up positive, indicating that exposure to the virus had occurred. Although other occupations such as farm workers, laborers, utility workers, heating and plumbing contractors, and park service employees all have a slightly higher risk of rodent contact, similar testing for SNV antibodies failed to reveal any exposure.

STATISTICS OF HANTAVIRUS PULMONARY SYNDROME

Since 1993 when the Four Corners Outbreak occurred, there have been 396 reported cases (as of July 2005) of HPS (Figure 7.1). Of these, 36% have resulted in death. Although the majority of cases have been reported from rural areas in the western United States, some eastern and southern states have documented hantavirus as well. There is no preference of gender, race, or age for hantavirus infection. Examining the **demographics,** however, gives us a better picture of who is being affected at the greatest rate. It was found that 77% of cases have been in Caucasians. At 62%, men have a slightly higher infection rate

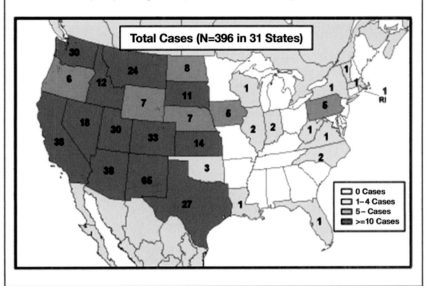

Figure 7.1 The prevalence of all HPS cases reported in the United States until July 6, 2005 as compiled by the CDC. The majority of hantavirus infections has been in the southwest U.S. and caused by the Sin Nombre strain.

than women. Additionally, the average age of an HPS patient was 38 years. The greatest number of cases occurred in the summer of 1993, when 48 cases were reported with a mortality rate approaching 60%.

If we examine demographics beyond overall numbers of cases in the United States, and look at state-to-state prevalence, we begin to see HPS "hot-spots" (see Figure 7.1). A study examined the incidence of HPS cases per state over the 12 years from 1993 to 2005. The highest incidences of HPS cases per 100,000 (rural population) were found, in decreasing order, in New Mexico, Utah, Nevada, Montana, Arizona, Colorado. New Mexico currently leads the country with 60 reported cases, which is more than double the number for every other reporting state except California and Arizona. Since New Mexico has a large rural population, the risk for rodent contact would be expected to be high; however, other factors are present. It is likely that mouse ecology and the drive for survival and shelter explain the high prevalence of HPS infection in these states. Four of the five states ranked highest in HPS incidence have arid climates with little rainfall. The deer mouse can survive in desert environments, but human settlements offer a more hospitable habitat. Outbuildings provide shelter from the sun and act as a secure nesting environment, while food stores guarantee survival. Perhaps in the most severe climates rodents actively seek out human habitation because, near humans, food and shelter is assured. This in turn puts humans at a higher risk of viral exposure and might explain the higher than average prevalence of HPS seen in the southwestern United States.

A GLOBAL PRESENCE

Hantaviruses have a longstanding global history. Old World viruses cause HFRS and their New World counterparts cause HPS. Europe, Scandinavia, Asia, and the Americas have histories of hantavirus infection and human disease. No documented cases of hantavirus have been reported in Africa, although rodents of the Muridae family are present. Australia and Antarctica are free of hantaviruses, which is probably due to the lack of indigenous Muricae rodents.

HPS has only been described in the Americas, although it is more common in South America. Cases have been reported in Argentina, Chile, Uruguay, Paraguay, Brazil, and Bolivia and are associated with many hantavirus species such as Andes, Bermejo, Laguna Negra, and the Pergamino viruses. In 1999, an outbreak of HPS in Panama was the first identified in Central America. The name of the viral species responsible for the outbreak was the Choclo virus and was transmitted by the pygmy rice rat *(Oligoryzomys fulvescens)*. Outbreaks in the United States have been well documented by the CDC; the primary virus responsible is the Sin Nombre virus. Some hantavirus species in the United States, such as the Prospect Hill virus, have not been directly linked with the ability to cause disease. Other viral species such as the New York, Monongahela, Bayou, and Black Creek viruses have all caused at least one HPS outbreak in the United States or Canada. As recently as the spring of 2005, several cases of hantavirus infection were reported in Alberta, Canada. When deer mice were subsequently tested in this region, 50% were shown to be hantavirus carriers in the area where the outbreak occurred.

The divergence of hantavirus diseases from HFRS to HPS lies with the rodent reservoirs. Hantaviruses generally infect rodents from the Muridae family that are found in Europe, Asia, and the Americas. Subfamilies include Murinae and Arvicolinae (Old World virus hosts) and Sigmdontinae (New World virus hosts). The subfamily Murinae are reservoirs for Hantaan, Dobrava, and Seoul viruses, which all cause HFRS. Arvicolinae, the host for Puumala virus, are voles and are primarily localized in Europe. Sigmodontinae carry the Sin Nombre virus as well as the other hantaviruses responsible for HPS.

Old World hantaviruses can cause severe to mild clinical presentations of HFRS depending on the infecting species. The Puumala virus, for example, causes a mild form of HFRS called nephropathia epidemica (less than 1% fatality rate) and has a high prevalence in Scandinavia. Severe HFRS, characterized by hemorrhages and renal failure, is usually attributed to infection with Dobrava or Hantaan viruses. Asia and Europe see a spike in reported cases in the spring and summer much like that seen with HPS in the Americas. Again, this is associated with agriculture and planting/harvesting schedules. Every year, Europe and Asia have high numbers of HFRS reported with varying severity. Nephropathia epidemica is primarily reported in Scandinavia, western Russia, and central Europe. Specifically, although

MICROARRAY AND HANTAVIRUS DETECTION

A microarray is a relatively new technology that is used to analyze gene expression. For example, one might use a microarray to compare the genes expressed in a normal cell versus a cancer cell. Another example might be if one wanted to examine whether genes were silenced after the treatment of a particular drug. Microarrays are very useful in that they are exquisitely sensitive, a lot of information can be gained from one experiment, and very little cellular material is required. So how exactly does this work? Microarrays are usually set up on microscope slides where thousands of tiny dots of DNA are spotted onto the glass. Each DNA spot represents a specific gene. Cellular samples are taken and the messenger RNA (mRNA) is extracted. One set of samples (Sample A) has the mRNA labeled with a green fluorescent dye and the second set of samples tested (Sample B) may be labeled with a red fluorescent dye. These samples are then incubated with the DNA spotted glass slide. If the mRNA matches the DNA probe, they will bind together very tightly. Once the array is read, one might see a green dot (sample A is making that mRNA), a red dot (only sample B is making that mRNA), or a yellow dot (both samples A and B are producing the mRNA). In this way, one can determine the particular activity of a gene in response to disease time, a drug, or any other parameter being tested. One new application for microarrays has been in the identification of hantavirus species. This technique is able to discriminate between those viruses causing HPS and HFRS even though very small genomic differences may be present. Using microarrays in this way would allow for a rapid screening of hantaviruses found in the wild to identify viral range, as well as new species that have not yet been identified.

Reference: Nordstrom H, et al. *J. Med Virol.* 2004, 72(4):646-55.

Sweden, Finland, and Norway combined report just over 1000 cases, Russia reports approximately 10,000 cases annually. The more severe form of HFRS associated with the Hantaan virus is reported primarily from China and eastern Russia, with a very high incidence of about 200,000 cases per year. Taken together, the presence of hantavirus species has a global reach. Our advances in technology and medicine have only now enabled us to identify these viruses as the cause of disease, but they have undoubtedly been present throughout history. As human populations continue to expand across the world and rodent contact becomes unavoidable, we may identify new strains of hantavirus causing both HPS and HFRS.

8

Preventing Exposure

Imagine that, while cleaning out the basement, you came across a nest, droppings, or some other sign of rodent infestation. What would you do? After school, you decide to fix a snack and, while looking through boxes of macaroni and cheese in your kitchen pantry, you discover evidence of gnawing on several containers. How do you proceed? During a camping trip, you return to a family cabin that has been closed up for the winter and find that mice have taken up residence. Do you pack up and go home? HPS has emerged as a result of infection with a New World hantavirus over the last decade. Although exposure to this class of virus can result in a high mortality rate, we are constantly learning more about how to fight infection and most importantly how to prevent exposure. We know the reservoir of hantavirus is the deer mouse or other related rodents and we now understand that the virus is usually inhaled to cause disease. The following section lists preventive measures to avoid rodent contact and describes how to safely clean an area that may have been contaminated.

LIMITING INDOOR EXPOSURE

Only a few rodent species have been identified as carriers of hantavirus strains that cause HPS. Unfortunately, these species' habitats encompass much of North and South America. Whether one's residence is in the city or country, there is always the possibility for rodent infestation. The first rule of rodent prevention is to reduce the availability of food sources. Keeping a home free of spilled food, open storage containers, or trash can help ensure that rodents are not lured into the building. If the rodent does not smell food, it will not be attracted. To minimize indoor rodent exposure, the CDC has set up the following basic rules:

- All food and water (including pet food) should be stored within thick plastic or metal containers with secure lids.

- All dishes, cooking utensils, and kitchenware should be washed after use and food remnants should be thrown away.

- Trash should be removed from the home on a regular basis and trash containers should be made of metal or a durable plastic with a secure fitting lid.

Another measure to prevent rodent infestation is to block entrances that lead to the exterior of the home. Small holes or gaps that may be found, such as those associated with plumbing or under cabinets, should be sealed off with such materials as steel wool or caulk. Metal flashing or gravel around the outside of the house can also prevent rodent entry. The yard should be kept free of unnecessary clutter, grass and shrubbery should be trimmed, and wood should not be stacked directly against the house. These measures discourage rodents from nesting near, if not in, one's home. Finally, spring-loaded snap traps should be used in areas around the home where rodents may find shelter. Traps that use an adhesive or that are designed to capture the rodent alive should be avoided, as viral shedding can continue through excreta (Figure 8.1).

LIMITING OUTDOOR EXPOSURE

Any time rodents and their excreta can come in contact with humans, the possibility for viral transmission exists. Whether one is setting up a tent in the woods, visiting a cabin that has been vacant for months, or simply taking in the view during a nature walk, there are certain precautions that should be taken to ensure contact with rodents is avoided. Not all types of rodents are carriers of hantavirus; nevertheless, it is safer to simply stay away from all signs of rodent inhabitation. Tents and sleeping bags should not be placed near rodent droppings,

The Prevention of Hantavirus Disease

Air out closed
buildings.
Disinfect places
rodents have been,
then clean up.

Repair screens
and holes
or cracks
in walls.

Wear rubber gloves.
Trap and disinfect rodents.

Disinfect and clean up rodent
nests and droppings.

Put materials
in 2 trash bags;
throw away,
burn or bury.

Formula for Disinfectant Solution:
1 and 1/2 cups of chlorine
bleach to every gallon of water.
Or use household spray disinfectant.

For more information, call your state health department. Or call CDC toll-free at 1-877-232-3322.

Figure 8.1 Several precautions can be taken to prevent possible exposure to rodents or their excreta during cleanup of rodent infected areas. Prevention of rodent infestation begins with sealing up holes and removal of trash and possible nesting sites such as woodpiles.

dens, burrows, or possible nesting areas such as garbage cans, woodpiles, or other sheltered areas. One also should never sleep on the bare ground; the use of a cot or elevated mattress, when possible, is preferable. To prevent rodents from visiting one's campsite, all food should be kept in closed containers and all garbage should be properly disposed in covered trash bins. Children should be warned to never play with or handle any rodents that they may see no matter how cute or friendly they appear.

Cabins that have not been in continual use should be aired out for 30 to 60 minutes prior to cleaning and disinfecting. Rodents often look for quiet shelter and the cabin should be inspected for signs of nests, droppings, and any material or food storage container that has been nibbled or gnawed upon. A 10% bleach solution is an effective disinfectant for durable surfaces such as floors and countertops and should be used in general cleaning. Water used for cooking, drinking, washing dishes, and brushing teeth should either be bottled or disinfected by a method such as boiling or filtration.

OCCUPATIONAL HAZARDS

There are many guidelines for preventing exposure to rodents possibly infected with hantavirus; however, certain individuals because of their occupations are at a higher risk of infection than the general public. Any time a person has regular contact with rodents or their habitat, extra precautions must be taken. Construction, utility workers, and pest-control workers may encounter rodents in vacant buildings, small crawl spaces, or unkempt basements. Those involved in construction projects involving the demolition or renovation of vacant, rodent-infested buildings should contact public health agencies for guidelines, as respirators may be required. Jobs related to agriculture and farming also pose an increased risk due to regular maintenance of outbuildings, barns, and storage facilities for grain or hay. The CDC has set the following precautions for those who are regularly exposed to rodents in hantavirus-affected areas:

- Workers must be informed of the symptoms of the disease and preventive measures to be taken.

- Workers should wear a half-face air-purifying respirator.

- Gloves should always be worn when handling and

disposing of rodents. Before removing gloves they should be thoroughly washed and disinfected before disposal.

- Any signs of respiratory illness within 45 days of exposure should be treated immediately and the physician informed of possible HPS transmission.

Although human-to-human transmission of hantavirus in North America has never been demonstrated, health care workers wear gowns and gloves as part of universal precautions. South America experienced an outbreak of Andes virus causing HPS that was spread through human contact. As a result, health care workers must also wear surgical masks and the patient must be confined to a private room. Those working in laboratories that process patient samples must follow Biosafety Level-2 (BSL-2) regulations. These include the use of gloves and a lab coat plus the disposal of all human waste products in biohazard trash that is incinerated. Additionally, if the manipulation of human body fluids can result in splatter or aerosolization, the use of a biological safety cabinet is also implemented. Basic research on hantaviruses that are grown in cell culture must be done in accordance with a higher safety level known as BSL-3. In addition to all of the standard precautions of BSL-2, a biosafety cabinet with an exhaust and ventilation system must be used, doors must be kept closed during experiments, respirators and face shields have to be worn, and decontamination of the area is completed daily. If proper precautions are followed, the risk of employee exposure to hantavirus or the rodent carrier can be minimized.

GENERAL SAFETY PRECAUTIONS AND RODENT CLEANUP

If rodent cleanup must be performed, there are many guidelines for safety (Figure 8.2). Remembering that hantavirus is transmitted by aerosolization from rodent excreta, precautions must be taken to prevent inhalation of any dried material. The following lists CDC guidelines for safe rodent cleanup depending on the material that has been contaminated:

Cleaning an Area of Rodent Excreta

1. Wear Gloves

2. Never use a vacuum cleaner or broom, as this will disperse aerosols.

3. Wet area and droppings with a solution of 10% bleach to disinfect.

BIOSAFETY LEVELS (BSL)

Those that work in research laboratories run the risk of becoming infected by the pathogens they culture. Of course, each pathogen carries a different degree of risk to its handler—e.g., *E.coli* is less pathogenic than hantavirus. In order to protect scientists and medical technicians from infectious agents, a set of standard protocols has been designed to reduce the risk of pathogen exposure. These can be divided into biosafety levels (BSL) of 1-4.

BSL-1 is the appropriate level to work under if the micro-organisms that are used do not cause disease in healthy humans and the agents are not considered hazardous. Work is done on standard benchtops, so doors should be kept closed during experiments. Gloves are recommended as well as lab coats and hands should always be washed after an experiment. Eating and drinking are not permitted.

BSL-2 is the level used when working with agents that pose a moderate risk to both employees and the environment. Handling specific pathogens such as the hepatitis virus requires previous vaccination. All employees are trained and wear protective equipment as needed. The laboratory

4. Clean up with a wet towel and mop area with 10% bleach solution.

5. Disinfect gloves before taking them off and then wash hands with soap and warm water.

Disposing of Dead Rodents

1. Spray rodent with disinfectant or 10% bleach solution.

2. Double bag the rodent.

is kept closed at all times. Infectious material must be properly separated and disposed in biohazard waste containers, with particular care being taken with sharp waste. All waste must be autoclaved to kill any pathogen and if aerosols are generated, a biosafety cabinet should be used.

BSL-3 follows all the rules of BSL-1 and BSL-2 with additional guidelines. This level is set up for those working with agents that can cause serious or possibly lethal disease if exposure occurs by inhalation. These laboratories are housed in special buildings designed to have filtered air-flow in biosafety chambers. Respirators must be worn and the lab is only accessible to appropriate personnel.

BSL-4 is designed for the most severe of all pathogens. This safety rating is for those working on deadly pathogens for which there is no cure and no vaccine. All personnel must wear protective suits with separate airflow. This serves to keep the scientist fully protected from the environment and the virus that is being cultured. The scientist must be fully decontaminated before leaving the laboratory.

Hantavirus Pulmonary Syndrome (HPS)

SEAL UP!
HOW TO KEEP RODENTS OUT OF YOUR HOME

- ☐ Seal up gaps around roofing, attic spaces, windows and doors.
- ☐ Examine the outside of your house for gaps between the foundation and the ground.
- ☐ Inspect for gaps under the sink and locations where water pipes come into your home.
- ☐ Check around vents and air conditioners for holes.
- ☐ Seal any gaps or holes with steel wool, lath metal or caulk.

TRAP UP!
HOW TO USE SNAP TRAPS

- ☐ Fix gaps in trailer skirting.
- ☐ Select an appropriate trap - some are for mice and some are for rats.
- ☐ Read the instructions on the box before setting the snap trap. Set away from children and pets.
- ☐ Place chunky peanut butter the size of a pea on the bait pan on the snap trap.
- ☐ Position the bait end of the trap next to the wall so it forms a "T" with the wall.
- ☐ Place snap traps in areas where you have seen rodents, nesting materials, urine or droppings.

CLEAN UP!
HOW TO KEEP A CLEAN AND HEALTHY HOME

How to clean up rodents and rodent droppings:

- ☐ Wear rubber or plastic gloves when handling dead rodents or rodent droppings.
- ☐ Spray dead rodent, urine or droppings with a disinfectant or a mixture of bleach and water.
- ☐ Soak rodent, nesting materials or droppings in solution for five minutes before wiping up with paper towel or rag as appropriate.
- ☐ Place the paper towel and rodent with trap or nesting material in a plastic bag and seal it.
- ☐ Place the full bag in a second plastic bag and seal it.
- ☐ Mop or sponge the area with a disinfectant or bleach solution.
- ☐ Wash gloved hands with soap and water or spray a disinfectant or bleach solution on gloves before taking them off.
- ☐ Wash hands with soap and warm water after taking off your gloves.

Clean up rodent food sources and nesting sites

- ☐ Place human and pet food in thick plastic or metal containers with tight lids.
- ☐ Wash dishes and cooking utensils soon after use.
- ☐ Put pet food away in rodent-proof containers after use. Do not leave pet-food or water bowls out overnight.
- ☐ Place garbage in thick plastic or metal can with a tight lid.
- ☐ Move woodpiles and composting bins more than 100 feet from the home.
- ☐ Trim grass and shrubbery within 100 feet of the home.

Prevention Checklist

CDC
CENTERS FOR DISEASE
CONTROL AND PREVENTION

Figure 8.2 The CDC has established guidelines for preventing hantavirus pulmonary syndrome. Their checklist includes directions for protecting your home from rodents, safely eliminating rodents with the use of snap traps, and cleaning any rodent waste or contamination.

3. Bury or burn the rodent or contact your local or state health department with questions.

Washing Fabrics

1. Clothing or items made of fabric should be washed in detergent and bleached if possible.

2. Rugs and carpets should be steam cleaned or shampooed.

Miscellaneous

1. Countertops and cabinets can be decontaminated with 10% bleach or other household disinfectants.

2. If an item is delicate and cannot be washed (such as papers or books), the item should be placed in full sunlight for several hours or indoors for a week. After this time, the item should be wiped with a damp cloth that was soaked in water and disinfectant.

Prospects for the Future

HPS and the viral species that causes it were discovered just over a decade ago. From the beginning of the first outbreak, it was unclear why people were getting sick and the fear was that it could be highly contagious. No one understood if the cause of sickness was viral, bacterial, or chemical, and fear of a new epidemic spread. Since that time, many other people all over the United States have become infected, though the disease predominantly affected regions in the southwestern United States. Mortality rates have declined from an initial 60 to 70% to 36% in 12 years' time. We now know what viral strains are responsible, how they are transmitted, what their rodent hosts are, and what the clinical course of the infection is. Cellular and molecular biology have elucidated the basic mechanisms of viral entry, immune response, and how damage is done within the body. We have gained a wealth of information in very little time.

Doctors and those in the medical profession are aware of HPS and know the importance of such medical interventions as oxygen administration and early admittance into the hospital. Local and national health agencies have set up a network of informative websites and have effectively disseminated information to the public. Scientists are making great strides in understanding how hantaviruses work, in hopes of understanding how to stop them or develop effective vaccines against them. Research continues every day. A search for scientific literature on the MedLine/PubMed website, part of the National Center for Biotechnology Information, reveals that many researchers are actively pursuing these answers. For example, the keyword "hantavirus" results in over 2,000 research papers that have been published, whereas a more specific search on "hantavirus pulmonary syndrome" lists over 400 research papers.

These numbers are increasing all the time. We are gaining more knowledge about rodent habitats, how the virus is shed, how the virus infects cells, how the immune response is activated, and how we can eliminate infection.

We must be aware, however, that viruses hold many surprises for us. Just as in the case of the Andes virus and its spread by human contact, these viruses are always capable of change. Although hantaviruses have been around for a very long time, we are just beginning to see these viruses as we are now in closer contact with their rodent hosts and their habitats. As time goes on, we will undoubtedly uncover new viral strains capable of causing HPS, just as we will continue to identify new rodent reservoirs. As hantavirus infections are a global problem, anyone coming into contact with rodents while on vacation, in the military, or within their home in the United States or abroad must take precautions. There will continue to be outbreaks but we now know how to better treat infection and increase the odds of survival. We will proceed into the future continually unraveling the methods of viral pathogenesis and we will work toward better treatments and vaccines for tomorrow.

Glossary

Acquired Immunity—A reaction and memory of white blood cells to a new antigenic challenge.

Aerosolization—The distribution of virus into the air.

Antibody—A specialized protein produced from immune cells known as lymphocytes that recognize foreign antigens.

Antigen—Any foreign substance that elicits an immune response.

Arrhythmia—An irregular heartbeat.

Arthropods—A category of animals that have segmented bodies, such as insects, arachnids, and crustaceans.

Capillary—The smallest of all blood vessels, having a wall only one cell thick.

Capsid—The protective shell or coat of a virus.

Cardiopulmonary—Having to do with the heart and lungs.

Chemokine—Small secreted proteins that cause migration of white blood cells.

Chronic—Something that persists for an extended amount of time.

Convalescence—A period of time when the body recovers from a serious illness, surgical procedure, or injury.

Correlation—A statistical measure of how two or more things are related.

Cytokine—Small proteins that are secreted from cells that affect the behavior of other cells.

Cytopathic—Causing cellular damage.

Demographic—A particular characteristic of the population, such as age, employment, education, or location of residence.

DNA (Deoxyribonucleic acid)—A type of nucleic acid that encodes genetic information important for biological processes.

Edema—Swelling of tissue.

ELISA (Enzyme-linked immunosorbent assay)—A sensitive technique that uses antibodies to detect small quantities of protein.

Encapsidate—The process of viral assembly where the coat protein is added around genetic material.

Endemic—Occurring in a specific area or region of a country.

Endocytosis—The process by which cells engulf material.

Endosome—The vesicle formed from the plasma membrane that is internalized into the cell.

Endothelium—The specialized cells that line blood vessels.

Epidemiologist—A person who studies trends in the transmission and causes of disease.

Epidemiology—The study of the distribution of disease and of the factors that affect health and disease within certain populations.

Exponential—Increasing at a very fast rate.

Febrile—Having a fever.

Genome—The entire hereditary information of an organism contained within nucleic acid.

Glycoprotein—A protein that has sugar chains attached to it.

Guanosine—One of the nucleic acid subunits containing guanine.

Hemorrhagic—Producing profuse internal bleeding from ruptured blood vessels.

Humoral immunity—The part of the immune response that is mediated by the production of antibodies.

Hypotension—Having very low blood pressure.

Immunoblast—An immature, atypical lymphocyte.

Immunogen—Something that is able to stimulate an immune response.

Immunohistochemistry—Use of antibodies to detect a specific protein in a tissue section, such as by colorimetric visualization.

Immunologic memory—The ability of the immune system to immediately mount a response to an infectious agent because it has been previously encountered.

Immunopathologic—Damage to cells that is mediated by the immune system.

Infectious—Capable of being transmitted from one person to another.

Inflammation—The body's response to injury or acute infection.

Glossary

Innate immunity—Part of the immune system that is present from birth.

Inoculum—An amount of cells or virus particles that are used to begin a new cycle of growth.

Kilobase—A term that refers to the length of DNA or RNA (1 kilobase = 1,000 bases of nucleic acid).

Koch's postulates—The minimum requirements that describe an infectious particle.

Latent—Staying dormant for a certain amount of time before reactivation.

Leukocytosis—Having an increased number of white blood cells.

Ligand—Any molecule that is capable of binding to another molecule with specificity.

Lysosome—An organelle in a cell that has many enzymes capable of digesting biomolecules.

Lytic—Causing a rupture or destruction of a cell.

Morphology—The study of the shape and characteristics of a cell or organism.

Mortality—The rate of death that results from a specific cause.

Mutation—A random change in the nucleic acid composition of DNA.

Nephric—Having to do with the tubules of the kidney.

Neuron—The primary cells of the nervous system.

Neutrophil—The most numerous white blood cell involved in innate immunity.

Nonpathogenic—Not causing disease.

Nucleic acid—A complex chain of biochemicals that carry genetic information.

Pathogen—An infectious particle that can cause disease.

Pathogenic—Capable of causing disease.

Pathologist—A scientist who studies the cause or progression of disease.

Pathology—The study of the changes that take place during disease.

Perinuclear—Associated with or occurring around the nucleus of the cell.

Platelet—A cell in the blood that is involved in clotting.

Polymerase—An enzyme that assembles nucleic acids together.

Polymerase chain reaction (PCR)—A process that amplifies the number of copies of a particular piece of DNA.

Prodrome—The early stages and signs of disease.

Proteases—Enzymes capable of breaking down protein.

Protein—A polymer of amino acids joined together in a specific order.

Pulmonary—Concerning or affecting the lungs.

Pyrogenic—Having the ability to cause fever.

Receptor—A specialized protein found on cell membranes that specifically binds to or interacts with another biological entity.

Renal—Referring or relating to the kidney.

Reservoir—Any person, animal, place, or substance in or on which an infectious agent lives.

Respiratory—Relating to the function of breathing.

RNA (Ribonucleic acid)—A type of nucleic acid that is important for transmission of genetic information, but also can have structural and enzymatic functions.

Taxonomy—A classification system for separation and organization within a group or population.

Thrombocytopenia—Having a low number of platelets in the blood.

Transcriptase—An enzyme that is capable of converting one type of nucleic acid to another.

Tropism—The specificity of a virus to infect its host cell.

Vascularized—Having many blood vessels.

Virulent—The ability to cause damage to a host.

Virus—An infectious particle consisting of a protein coat that surrounds nucleic acid.

Bibliography

Armstrong, L. R., S. R. Zaki, M. J. Goldoft, R. L. Todd, A. S. Khan, R. F. Khabbaz, T. G. Ksiazek, and C. J. Peters. "Hantavirus Pulmonary Syndrome Associated With Entering or Cleaning Rarely Used, Rodent-Infested Structures." *J Infect Dis* 172(1995): 1166.

Bharadwaj, M., K. Mirowsky, C. Ye, J. Botten, B. Masten, J. Yee, C. R. Lyons, and B. Hjelle. "Genetic Vaccines Protect Against Sin Nombre Hantavirus Challenge in the Deer Mouse *(Peromyscus maniculatus)*." *J Gen Virol* 83(2002): 1745–1751.

Bharadwaj, M., R. Nofchissey, D. Goade, F. Koster, and B. Hjelle. "Humoral Immune Responses in the Hantavirus Cardiopulmonary Syndrome." *J Infect Dis* 182(2000): 43–48.

Botten, J., K. Mirowsky, C. Ye, K. Gottlieb, M. Saavedra, L. Ponce, and B. Hjelle. "Shedding and Intracage Transmission of Sin Nombre Hantavirus in the Deer Mouse *(Peromyscus maniculatus)* Model." *J Virol* 76(2002): 7587–7594.

Centers for Disease Control and Prevention. *Hantavirus Pulmonary Syndrome (HPS): 1996 Case Definition.* Atlanta, GA: U.S. Department of Health and Human Services, CDC, 2004.

Centers for Disease Control and Prevention. "Hantavirus Pulmonary Syndrome—Colorado and New Mexico, 1998." *MMWR* 47(1998): 449–452.

Centers for Disease Control and Prevention. "Hantavirus Pulmonary Syndrome—United States: Updated Recommendations for Risk." *MMWR* 51(2002): 1–12.

Childs, J.E., T. G. Ksiazek, C. F. Spiropoulou, J. W. Krebs, S. Morzunov, G. O. Maupin, K. L. Gage, et al. "Serologic and Genetic Identification of *Peromyscus maniculatus* as the Primary Rodent Reservoir for a New Hantavirus in the Southwestern United States." *J Infect Dis* 169(1994): 1271–1280.

Clement, J. P. "Hantavirus." *Antiviral Res* 57(2003): 121–127.

Douglass, R. J., C. H. Calisher, and K. C. Bradley. "State-by-State Incidences of Hantavirus Pulmonary Syndrome in the United States, 1993–2004." *Vector Borne Zoonotic Dis* 5(2005): 189–192.

Douglass, R. J., A. J. Kuenzi, C. Y. Williams, S. J. Douglass, and J. N. Mills. "Removing Deer Mice From Buildings and the Risk for Human Exposure to Sin Nombre Virus." *Emerg Infect Dis* 9(2003): 390–392.

Duchin, J. S., F. T. Koster, C. J. Peters, G. L. Simpson, B. Tempest, S. R. Zaki, and T. G. Ksiazek, et al. "Hantavirus Pulmonary Syndrome: A Clinical Description of 17 Patients With a Newly Recognized Disease." *N Engl J Med* 330(1994): 949–955.

Fields, Bernard N., David M. Knipe, and Peter M. Howley. *Fundamental Virology*. Philadelphia, PA: Lippincott–Raven, 1996.

Goldsmith, C. S., L. H. Elliott, C. J. Peters, and S. R. Zaki. "Ultrastructural Characteristics of Sin Nombre Virus, Causative Agent of Hantavirus Pulmonary Syndrome." *Arch Virol* 140(1995): 2107–2122.

Pan American Health Organization. *Hantavirus in the Americas: Guidelines for Diagnosis, Treatment, Prevention, and Control*. Washington, D.C.: PAHO, 1999.

Hjelle, B., S. Jenison, G. Mertz, F. Koster, and K. Foucar. "Emergence of Hantaviral Disease in the Southwestern United States." *West J Med* 161(1994): 467–473.

Hooper, J. W., T. Larsen, D. M. Custer, and C. S. Schmaljohn. "A Lethal Disease Model for Hantavirus Pulmonary Syndrome." *Virology* 289(2001): 6–14.

Horgan, J. "The No-Name Virus: Questions Linger After the Four Corners Outbreak." *Sci Am* 271(1994): 34–36.

Huggins, J.W., C. M. Hsiang, T. M. Cosgriff, M. Y. Guang, J. I. Smith, Z. O. Wu, J. W. LeDuc, et al. "Prospective, Double-Blind, Concurrent, Placebo-Controlled Clinical Trial of Intravenous Ribavirin Therapy of Hemorrhagic Fever With Renal Syndrome." *J Infect Dis* 164(1991): 1119–1127.

Hutchinson, K.L., C. J. Peters, and S. T. Nichol. "Sin Nombre Virus mRNA Synthesis." *Virology* 224(1996): 139–149.

Khaiboullina S.F., and S. C. St Jeor "Hantavirus Immunology." *Viral Immunol* 15(2002): 609–625.

Khan, A. S., R. F. Khabbaz, L. R. Armstrong, R. C. Holman, S. P. Bauer, J. Graber, T. Strine, et al. "Hantavirus Pulmonary Syndrome: The First 100 US Cases." *J Infect Dis* 173(1995): 1297–1303.

Khan, A. S., T. G. Ksiazek, and C. J. Peters. "Hantavirus Pulmonary Syndrome." *Lancet* 347(1996): 739–741.

Bibliography

Koster, F., K. Foucar, B. Hjelle, A. Scott, Y. Y. Chong, R. Larson, and M. McCabe. "Rapid Presumptive Diagnosis of Hantavirus Cardiopulmonary Syndrome by Peripheral Blood Smear Review." *Am J Clin Pathol* 116(2001): 665–672.

Ksiazek, T. G., S. T. Nichol, J. N. Mills, M. G. Groves, A. Wozniak, S. McAdams, M. C. Monroe, et al. "Isolation, Genetic Diversity, and Geographic Distribution of Bayou Virus (Bunyaviridae: Hantavirus)." *Am J Trop Med Hyg* 57(1997): 445–448.

Larson, R. S., D. C. Brown, C. Ye, and B. Hjelle. "Peptide Antagonists That Inhibit Sin Nombre Virus and Hantaan Virus Entry Through the Beta3-Integrin Receptor." *J Virol* 79(2005): 7319–7326.

Lednicky, J. A. "Hantaviruses. A Short Review." *Arch Pathol Lab Med* 127(2003): 30–35.

Lee, H. W., P. W. Lee, and K. M. Johnson. "Isolation of the Etiologic Agent of Korean Hemorrhagic Fever. 1978." *J Infect Dis* 190(2004): 1711–1721.

Le Guenno, B. "Emerging Viruses." *Sci Am* 273(1995): 56–64.

Maes, P., J. Clement, I. Gavrilovskaya, and M. Van Ranst. "Hantaviruses: Immunology, Treatment, and Prevention." *Viral Immunol* 17(2004): 481–497.

Marshall, E. "Hantavirus Outbreak Yields to PCR." *Science* 262(1993): 832, 834–836.

Miedzinski, L. "Community-Acquired Pneumonia: New Facets of an Old Disease—Hantavirus Pulmonary Syndrome." *Respir Care Clin N Am* 11(2005): 45–58.

Mills J.N., T. G. Ksiazek, B. A. Ellis, P. E. Rollin, S. T. Nichol, T. L. Yates, W. L. Gannon, et al. "Patterns of Association With Host and Habitat: Antibody Reactive With Sin Nombre Virus in Small Mammals in the Major Biotic Communities of The Southwestern United States." *Am J Trop Med Hyg* 56(1997): 273–284.

Nichol, S.T., C. F. Spiropoulou, S. Morzunov, P. E. Rollin, T. G. Ksiazek, H. Feldmann, A. Sanchez, J. Childs, S. Zaki, and C. J. Peters. "Genetic Identification Of A Hantavirus Associated With An Outbreak Of Acute Respiratory Illness." *Science* 262(1993): 914–917.

Niikura, M., A. Maeda, T. Ikegami, M. Saijo, I. Kurane, and S. Morikawa. "Modification of Endothelial Cell Functions by Hantaan Virus Infection:

Prolonged Hyper-Permeability Induced by TNF-Alpha of Hantaan Virus-Infected Endothelial Cell Monolayers." *Arch Virol* 149(2004): 1279–1292.

Nolte, K. B., R. M. Feddersen, K. Foucar, S. R. Zaki, F. T. Koster, D. Madar, T. L. Merlin, P. J. McFeeley, E. T. Umland, and R. E. Zumwalt. "Hantavirus Pulmonary Syndrome in the United States: A Pathological Description of a Disease Caused by a New Agent." *Hum Pathol* 26(1995): 110–120.

Nordstrom, H., P. Johansson, Q. G. Li, A. Lundkvist, P. Nilsson, and F. Elgh. "Microarray Technology for Identification and Distinction of Hantaviruses." *J Med Virol* 72(2004): 646–655.

Pensiero, M. N., J. B. Sharefkin, C. W. Dieffenbach, and J. Hay. "Hantaan Virus Infection of Human Endothelial Cells." *J Virol.* 66(1992): 5929–5936.

Peters, C. J., and A. S. Khan. "Hantavirus Pulmonary Syndrome: The New American Hemorrhagic Fever." *Clin Infect Dis* 34(2002): 1224–1231.

Peters, C. J., A. S. Khan, and S. R. Zaki. "Hantaviruses in the United States." *Arch Intern Med* 156(1996): 705–707.

Peters C. J., G. L. Simpson, and H. Levy. "Spectrum of Hantavirus Infection: Hemorrhagic Fever With Renal Syndrome and Hantavirus Pulmonary Syndrome." *Annu Rev Med* 50(1999): 531–545.

Rollin, P. E., T. G. Ksiazek, L. H. Elliott, E. V. Ravkov, M. L. Martin, S. Morzunov, W. Livingstone, et al. "Isolation of Black Creek Canal Virus, a New Hantavirus From *Sigmodon hispidus* in Florida." *J Med Virol* 46(1995): 35–39.

Schmaljohn, C., and B. Hjelle. "Hantaviruses: A Global Disease Problem." *Emerging Infectious Diseases* 3(1997): 95–104.

Simonsen, L., M. J. Dalton, R. F. Breiman, T. Hennessy, E. T. Umland, C. M. Sewell, P. E. Rollin, T. G. Ksiazek, and C. J. Peters. "Evaluation of the Magnitude of the 1993 Hantavirus Outbreak in the Southwestern United States." *J Infect Dis* 172(1995): 729–733.

Song, J. W., L. J. Baek, D. C. Gajdusek, R. Yanagihara, I. Gavrilovskaya, B. J. Luft, E. R. Mackow, and B. Hjelle. "Isolation of Pathogenic Hantavirus From White-Footed Mouse (*Peromyscus leucopus*) [Letter]". *Lancet* 344(1994): 1637.

Spiropoulou, C. F., C. S. Goldsmith, T. R. Shoemaker, C. J. Peters, and R. W. Compans. "Sin Nombre Virus Glycoprotein Trafficking." *Virology* 308(2003): 48–63.

Bibliography

Susman, E. "Haemorrhagic Viruses as Bioweapons." *Lancet Infect Dis* 1(2001): 289.

Tamura M, Asada H, Kondo K, Takahashi M, Yamanishi K. "Effects of human and murine interferons against hemorrhagic fever with renal syndrome (HFRS) virus (Hantaan virus)." *Antiviral Res.* 8(1987):171-8.

Toro, J., J. D. Vega, A. S. Khan, J. N. Mills, P. Padula, W. Terry, Z. Yadon, et al. "An Outbreak of Hantavirus Pulmonary Syndrome, Chile, 1997." *Emerg Infect Dis* 4(1998): 687–694.

Tsai, T. F. "Hemorrhagic Fever With Renal Syndrome: Mode of Transmission to Humans." *Lab Anim Sci* 37(1987): 428–430.

Vitek C. R., R. F. Breiman, T. G. Ksiazek, P. E. Rollin, J. C. McLaughlin, E. T. Umland, K. B. Nolte, A. Loera, C. M. Sewell, and C. J. Peters. "Evidence Against Person-to-Person Transmission of Hantavirus to Health Care Workers." *Clin Infect Dis* 22(1996): 824–826.

Wells, R. M., S. S. Estani, Z. E. Yadon, D. Enria, P. Padula, N. Pini, J. N. Mills, C. J. Peters, E. L. Segura, and the Hantavirus Pulmonary Syndrome Study Group for Patagonia. "An Unusual Hantavirus Outbreak in Southern Argentina: Person-to-Person Transmission?" *Emerging Infectious Diseases* 3(1997): 171–174.

Wells, R. M., J. Young, R. J. Williams, L. R. Armstrong, K. Busico, A. S. Khan, T. G. Ksiazek, et al. "Hantavirus Transmission in the United States." *Emerg Infect Dis* 3(1997): 361–365.

Wrobel, S. "Serendipity, Science, and a New Hantavirus." *FASEB J.* 9(1995): 1247–1254. Erratum in: *FASEB J.* 10(1996): 178.

Yanagihara, R., and D. J. Silverman. "Experimental Infection of Human Vascular Endothelial Cells by Pathogenic and Nonpathogenic Hantaviruses." *Arch Virol* 111(1990): 281–286.

Young, J. C., G. R. Hansen, T. K. Graves, M. P. Deasy, J. G. Humphreys, C. L. Fritz, K. L. Gorham, et al. "The Incubation Period of Hantavirus Pulmonary Syndrome." *Am J Trop Med Hyg* 62(2000): 714–717.

Zaki, S. R., A. S. Khan, R. A. Goodman, L. R. Armstrong, P. W. Greer, L. M. Coffield, T. G. Ksiazek, P. E. Rollin, C. J. Peters, and R. F. Khabbaz. "Retrospective Diagnosis of Hantavirus Pulmonary Syndrome, 1978–1993: Implications for Emerging Infectious Diseases." *Arch Pathol Lab Med* 120(1996): 134–139.

Zaki, S.R., P. W. Greer, L. M. Coffield, C. S. Goldsmith, K. B. Nolte, K. Foucar, R. M. Feddersen, R. E. Zumwalt, G. L. Miller, A. S. Khan, et al. "Hantavirus Pulmonary Syndrome. Pathogenesis of an Emerging Infectious Disease." *Am J Pathol* 146(1995): 552–579.

Zeitz, P. S., J. M. Graber, R. A. Voorhees, C. Kioski, L. A. Shands, T. G. Ksiazek, S. Jenison, and R. F. Khabbaz. "Assessment of Occupational Risk for Hantavirus Infection in Arizona and New Mexico." *J Occup Environ Med* 39(1997): 463–467.

Further Reading

Garrett, Laurie. *The Coming Plague: Newly Emerging Diseases in a World Out of Balance.* New York, NY: Penguin, 1995.

Harper, David R., and Andrea S. Meyer. *Of Mice, Men, and Microbes: Hantavirus.* San Diego, CA: Academic Press, 1999.

Le Guenno, B. "Emerging Viruses." *Sci Am* 273(1995): 56–64.

Lednicky, J. A. "Hantaviruses. A Short Review." *Arch Pathol Lab Med* 127(2003): 30–35.

Marshall, E. "Hantavirus Outbreak Yields to PCR." *Science* 262(1993): 832, 834–836.

Wrobel, S. "Serendipity, Science, and a New Hantavirus." *FASEB J* (1995): 1247–1254.

Websites

www.cdc.gov/hantavirus

www.cdc.gov/ncidod

www.emedicine.com
(search for "hantavirus pulmonary syndrome")

www.virology.net/garryfavwebindex.html

www.osha.gov
(search for "hantavirus")

www.faseb.org/opa/hanta.html

www.lungusa.org
(search for "hantavirus pulmonary syndrome")

www.montana.edu
(search for "hantavirus")

www.nlm.nih.gov/medlineplus/
(search for "hantavirus")

http://earthobservatory.nasa.gov/Study/Hanta/

Index

Picture Credits

11: © Scherer Illustrations
13: © Courtesy Public Health Image Library (PHIL), CDC /James Gathary
15: © Courtesy of CDC
16: © Courtesy of CDC
19: © Courtesy of CDC
23: © Courtesy Public Health Image Library (PHIL), CDC/ Cynthia Goldsmith
24: © Scherer Illustrations
25: © Scherer Illustrations
33: © Dr. Dennis Kunkrl/ Visuals Unlimited
35: © Scherer Illustrations
41: © Peter Lamb
46: © Scherer Illustrations

Cover: © Courtesy of CDC

52: (top) © Courtesy Public Health Image Library (PHIL), CDC
52: (bottom) © Courtesy Public Health Image Library (PHIL), CDC/ James Gathany
55: © Scherer Illustrations
60: © Scherer Illustrations
65: (top)© Courtesy Public Health Image Library (PHIL), CDC/ D. Loren Ketai, M.D.
65: (bottom)© Courtesy Public Health Image Library (PHIL), CDC/ D. Loren Ketai, M.D
70: © Courtesy of CDC
77: © Courtesy of CDC
82: © Courtesy of CDC

About the Author

Stephanie J. Leuenroth grew up in both Smithtown and New Windsor, New York. She earned a B.S. degree in biotechnology from Rochester Institute of Technology in 1995, and then went on to earn a Ph.D. in pathobiology from Brown University in 2000. While in graduate school, she studied inflammation as it relates to the regulation and function of the human neutrophil. Disease implications included respiratory distress syndromes, bacterial sepsis, and shock. She was awarded an American Cancer Society Postdoctoral fellowship while working at Yale University in 2001. Her work has focused on natural product mode-of-action studies with disease implications into cancer, arthritis, and autoimmunity. Presently, she is an Associate Research Scientist at Yale University and plans to pursue a career in disease research and drug development. She is currently living in Hope Valley, Rhode Island with her husband.

About the Founding Editor

The late **I. Edward Alcamo** was a Distinguished Teaching Professor of Microbiology at the State University of New York at Farmingdale. Alcamo studied biology at Iona College in New York and earned his M.S. and Ph.D. degrees in microbiology at St. John's University, also in New York. He had taught at Farmingdale for over 30 years. In 2000, Alcamo won the Carski Award for Distinguished Teaching in Microbiology, the highest honor for microbiology teachers in the United States. He was a member of the American Society for Microbiology, the National Association of Biology Teachers, and the American Medical Writers Association. Alcamo authored numerous books on the subjects of microbiology, AIDS, and DNA technology as well as the award-winning textbook *Fundamentals of Microbiology*, now in its sixth edition.